Praise for *It Takes*

I know countless families who have ask[...] was written, and that Brittany Salmon [...] brings difficulties and challenges. Transcultural adoptions can sometimes be even more confusing, for parents and children and birth families, all wanting to love each other and to do the right thing. This book raises difficult questions, offers authentic reflection, and can help families think through how best to approach these matters. It takes more than love, but it takes nothing less. This is a book of love and of hope.

RUSSELL MOORE, author, *Christianity Today*'s chair of public theology, and director of the Public Theology Project

For anyone with even a passing interest in transracial adoption, this book is required reading. As someone who has been personally and professionally involved with adoption for twenty-five years, I only wish this book had been available decades ago. Brittany addresses core, significant issues with clarity and grace—and a holistic gospel perspective anchored in love. This book will help countless children and families.

KELLY ROSATI, adoptive mom and child advocate

It Takes More Than Love is a wonderful resource for adoptive families, or anyone that knows an adoptive family! Brittany provides a compassionate, gospel-informed perspective on adoption with all of its complexity. This book, which beautifully incorporates perspectives from not only adoptive parents but also adoptees and birth parents, does a marvelous job highlighting the inherent dignity and worth of every person. What a gift.

LAUREN MCAFEE, cross-cultural adoptive mother; Ministry Coordinator, Hobby Lobby Corporate

Most parents would do anything to give their children the love they need. In *It Takes More Than Love*, Brittany Salmon equips not just parents but all of us to love transracial adoptees well. By listening to and elevating the voices of transracial adoptees, she identifies how a color-blind approach to adoption is harmful and provides action steps to better support transracial adoptees. Brittany shows how embracing God's beautiful, diverse design for people through gospel-centered antiracism work demonstrates to transracial adoptees that they are seen, known, and deeply loved.

NATHAN BULT, SVP of Public & Government Affairs at Bethany Christian Services

In *It Takes More Than Love*, Brittany navigates the nuances of adoption in a thoughtful way that honors adoptees, birth parents, and people who build their family through adoption. As an adoptee, I'm deeply grateful for Brittany's attention to issues of navigating trauma, the importance of representation, and race. This book is a vitally important resource for Christians stepping into complex spaces.

CHELSEA SOBOLIK, Director of Policy, Ethics and Religious Liberty Commission; author, *Longing for Motherhood*

It is tempting to think that if you just give a child a loving home and family that it will all work out and everyone would live happily ever after. This romantic ending only happens in fairy tales. Adoption is far more complex and unpredictable, yet worthy of pursuing all the ways possible to care for the orphan and oppressed. Brittany Salmon helps prospective and adoptive parents consider as well as prepare for the complexity of transracial and cross-cultural adoption, not only through the eyes of an adoptive parent, but through the often unheard voices of adoptees.

TONY MERIDA (pastor and author) **AND KIMBERLY MERIDA,** adoptive parents of five

Humble, honest, and insightful. With her eyes fixed on Jesus and her heart gripped by the gospel, Brittany provides an incredibly helpful guide on how to honor Christ in cross-cultural adoption. This book is a must-read for all who are involved in such adoptions.

BRYAN LORITTS, author, *The Dad Difference*

Joy and sorrow. Early in the book Brittany Salmon accurately uses that phrase to describe the juxtaposition that exists within cross-cultural adoption. Adoption matters, and it is beautiful, but we need to tell the whole story of adoption. We need to be honest about the complexities and the challenges. In this book, Salmon does just that, all while showing how we can honor God in the midst of our adoptive stories. I am glad to recommend this book as a resource for those who are involved in cross-cultural adoption.

MICAH FRIES, Director of Engagement, GlocalNet; Director of Programs, Multi-Faith Neighbors Network; author, *Leveling the Church*

As a cross-cultural adoptive mom, I wish I had had this book when we adopted over a decade ago. I will be giving it to all our adoptive friends plus those who love and support them. This is a rich resource for not only the adoptive family, but for their entire community. Brittany speaks from years of experience and education—she's a seasoned mom as well as a strong and gracious advocate for first moms and adopted children. She centers the right stories and the right wisdom. The adoption community has needed this book for far too long. I'm so glad to have it now.

JEN OSHMAN, author, *Enough about Me*

Love is required in any parent/child relationship, and Salmon offers tangible ways to express that love amid the complexities, joys, and sorrows of cross-cultural adoption. Anchored in Scripture, *It Takes More Than Love* offers adoptive parents, ministers, and friends a realistic yet hope-filled window into the trials and beauty of cross-cultural adoption underscored by proposing a biblical motivation and approach to inform this sacred journey to God's glory.

WALTER R. STRICKLAND II, Assistant Professor of Theology, Southeastern Seminary

I opened this book not knowing what to expect; to say I was pleasantly surprised is a gross understatement. It is impressive. Brittany is brilliant, speaks with candor, and is humble—and she has done her homework. Most importantly, she practices what she preaches. And while this is a book about cross-cultural adoption, I can't help but think it a primer for living wisely and faithfully in a multicultural country and church.

MARLENA GRAVES, author, *The Way Up Is Down: Becoming Yourself by Forgetting Yourself*

Brittany tackles a complex subject with so much wisdom, humility, and grace. It challenges you in personal and practical ways. Highly recommend for anyone considering adoption or who has been impacted by adoption in some way.

LAURA BRUDER, Executive Director of BraveLove

IT TAKES MORE THAN LOVE

A Christian Guide to Navigating the
Complexities of Cross-Cultural Adoption

BRITTANY SALMON

MOODY PUBLISHERS

CHICAGO

All Scripture quotations are taken from the Holy Bible, New International Version®, NIV®. Copyright ©1973, 1978, 1984, 2011 by Biblica, Inc.™ Used by permission of Zondervan. All rights reserved worldwide. www.zondervan.com The "NIV" and "New International Version" are trademarks registered in the United States Patent and Trademark Office by Biblica, Inc.™

All names and some details in the Adoptee Voice sections have been changed to protect privacy.

All emphasis to Scripture and to other citations has been added by the author.

Edited by Pamela Joy Pugh
Interior design: Ragont Design
Cover design: Christopher Tobias
Cover image of knot copyright © 2020 by New Africa / Adobe Stock (319376026). All rights reserved.

Library of Congress Cataloging-in-Publication Data

Names: Salmon, Brittany, author.
Title: It takes more than love : a Christian guide to navigating the complexities of cross-cultural adoption / Brittany Salmon.
Description: Chicago : Moody Publishers, [2022] | Includes bibliographical references. | Summary: "Brittany Salmon shares her family's story of transracial adoption and offers biblical guidance for others. No one is promising transracial adoption will be easy—least of all Brittany! Yet when an adoptive family honors the ethnicity of their children, they—and the watching world—will see God at work"—Provided by publisher.
Identifiers: LCCN 2021043342 (print) | LCCN 2021043343 (ebook) | ISBN 9780802424150 | ISBN 9780802499820 (ebook)
Subjects: LCSH: Interracial adoption. | Interracial adoption--Religious aspects--Christianity. | Race awareness. | Racially mixed families. | Adoptive parents. | Adopted children. | BISAC: FAMILY & RELATIONSHIPS / Multiracial Families | RELIGION / Christian Living / Parenting
Classification: LCC HV875.6 .S25 2022 (print) | LCC HV875.6 (ebook) | DDC 362.734089--dc23
LC record available at https://lccn.loc.gov/2021043342
LC ebook record available at https://lccn.loc.gov/2021043343

All websites listed herein are accurate at time of publication but may change in the future or cease to exist. The listing of websites and resources does not imply publisher endorsement of the site's entire contents. Groups and organizations are listed for informational purposes, and listing does not imply publisher endorsement of their activities.

Originally delivered by fleets of horse-drawn wagons, the affordable paperbacks from D. L. Moody's publishing house resourced the church and served everyday people. Now, after more than 125 years of publishing and ministry, Moody Publishers' mission remains the same—even if our delivery systems have changed a bit. For more information on other books (and resources) created from a biblical perspective, go to www.moodypublishers.com or write to:

Moody Publishers
820 N. LaSalle Boulevard
Chicago, IL 60610

1 3 5 7 9 10 8 6 4 2

Printed in the United States of America

For adoptive families everywhere.

May we know better and then do better for the good of our

children and for the glory of God.

Contents

PART 3: "WHEN YOU KNOW BETTER, DO BETTER"

Part 1

BOARDS FOR THE BRIDGE

CHAPTER 1

Welcome to
the Journey

I have a love/hate relationship with adoption.

I know, that is an odd sentence to start out an adoption book. And yet it's true. For a long time, I considered myself an adoption advocate. And yet, over the years I've found myself no longer comfortable with that label.

Do I earnestly believe that every child should have a safe and loving family? Yes, absolutely.

Do I believe that adoption is the only way to achieve that goal? No.

Do I believe that the best option is for children to be raised safely within their birth families and cultures? Of course.

Is that always an option? Sadly, no.

Do I love adoption for allowing me the incredible honor of parenting our children? Yes.

Do I hate the trauma and loss that adoption also brings? Yes.

The truth is, the longer I've been in the adoption world the more I've come to realize that adoption is complex. Rarely, in the adoption world, is it either/or; more often than not, it's both/and. And I think that's important to acknowledge up front, otherwise the rest of this book might not make sense when I acknowledge pain and trauma but also talk about joy and satisfaction and family.

After my husband, Ben, and I found out that we were pregnant with twins, I read everything I could get my hands on. I scoured the internet for resources on prematurity, NICU stays, identity development, how to tandem nurse, and so on. Once I got the basics down for keeping tiny humans alive, I started reading books on parenting, discipline strategies, discipling your children . . . you name it, I read about it.

When we started walking through our first adoption journey, I did the same thing. I checked out books from our library, joined online adoption forums, and read mommy blogs. One of the resources I wish I had was a book like the one you're reading right now.

Adoption is complex. It's joy and suffering and loss and gain and hope and disappointment all in one. From an adoptive parent standpoint, we gain a lot. But it needs to be said clearly that adoptees and birth families lose much during this process. Even when adoption is the best and most ethical option—even when a child gains a loving and wonderful family—he or she will still experience loss. When the adoption is cross-cultural, another layer of loss is added: loss of culture, language, and community. Please don't let those statements discourage you. We'll talk about all this in due time.

On our journey to adoption, I read a lot of perspectives, but none that made space for both the realities and hardships that adoption brings *and* the hope that we have *in all things*—even in really hard things—in Christ. Someone has said that if there's a book you want to read that doesn't yet exist, you need to write it. And so, this is why you're holding this book in your hands today. I firmly believe that we can hold sorrow and joy in the same hand. I believe we can have hope in the midst of hardship, and I believe that brokenness and celebration are all welcomed at the foot of the cross. And I want Christian adoptive families to have access to a guide that boldly proclaims the goodness and glory of God in both the messiness and beauty of our adoption journeys. And so, here it is.

IT'S BOTH/AND, NOT EITHER/OR

A year before our first children were born, dear friends were placed with a child via domestic infant adoption. Our friends are White, and they were placed with a beautiful Black little girl. She was a preemie, and I watched intently, not knowing that we would one day have preemies of our own.

When our preemie twins were about a year old, these friends encouraged us to consider domestic infant adoption. Depending on location, needs vary, but in our state there was a *long* list of White prospective adoptive parents only wanting White, healthy children. Our friend's agency was in need of families of any ethnicity to adopt non-White children, and even more specifically, we were told that Black male babies were the hardest to place. The number of families willing to adopt Black children was minuscule, and if the agency didn't have families to place these babies with, the children would then go into foster care. White children were placed quickly, while other BIPOC children went into a system (BIPOC stands for Black, Indigenous, People of Color).

Black expectant mothers who chose life for their children and wanted to choose a family for them didn't have the same plethora of families to choose from that White birth mothers had.

I learned of this and I was heartbroken. After all, of all the people in the world, Christians *should be* people who hold tightly to the tenets of our faith that all people are created in the image of God and, as such, should be treated equally. Surely we can agree that all children, of every ethnicity, should be treated fairly and have the same access to a safe and loving home. I believed that deep in my bones, and still do today.

Parenting transracially doesn't come naturally, nor does it just happen with time. It is hard work and yet—it's been one of the greatest blessings in our family's life.

So, after much praying and evaluation, we decided to adopt domestically and open our home to a child of any ethnicity. And we decided that we would be committed to learning about whatever cultural and ethnic history our child would bring to our family as we pressed into the adoption community.

Looking back, this was a sweet and hard season as many of my presuppositions about the sweetness and inherent goodness of adoption were challenged. I read adoptees' perspectives as well as birth parents' perspectives, and quickly realized that I was only looking at adoption from my point in the adoption triad (birth parent, adoptee, adoptive parent). Yes, we were growing our family. And yes, a child was gaining a new family, but that child had also lost something precious: their first family and culture. Yes, a birth mom was choosing life for a child, but she was also choosing life without her child. And the more I listened and learned, the more my heart was broken.

When we walked through adoption the first time, and I sat in a room holding a baby as another woman left the hospital with empty arms, I felt the juxtaposition acutely:

Joy and sorrow.

Loss and gain.

Broken and whole.

Grateful and devastated.

All of it wrapped up into one moment, one specific place and time. I'd like to share that one emotion trumped all the others, but truthfully, all of them were present on that day. We were in awe and smitten with our son, and we were simultaneously grieved at what he had lost, at what his birth mom had lost.

The beautiful narrative about adoption that I previously held wasn't fully untrue, but it wasn't the full truth either. Adoption *can* be beautiful, but only if that beauty makes room for joy and sorrow to sit together. With adoption, it has to be both/and, not either/or; otherwise you're missing the complete picture.

For my friends who pursued international adoption, their journeys were similar and yet also very different. Yes, their families grew through adoption, but their children suffered loss of family, culture, language, and roots. Some of their children had no remaining relatives, while others have some living relatives who were unable to care for them. And through international adoption, their children's connection to their cultural heritage was strained (at best) and severed (at worst).

Navigating how to parent well transracially has been a learning curve for us, just like much of any parenting is. Parenting transracially doesn't come naturally, nor does it just happen with time. It takes intentionality, listening, learning, growing, repenting, changing, and then repeating and starting over again. It is hard work and yet—it's been one of the greatest blessings in our family's life. Because we have chosen to be a multicultural family and to honor the ethnic heritages of our children, we've learned to navigate and celebrate the tensions a both/and life can bring. But as a result, we get to see and experience the beauty of a gloriously creative God.

A GUIDE FOR THE JOURNEY

Before we jump into the meat of the book, I wanted to take a moment to welcome you— wherever you are in the journey. The state of adoption has changed drastically in the United States and globally over the last few decades. As we grow and learn more about adoption practices, we can intentionally seek to do better, whether we're just beginning the adoption journey or we're seasoned adoptive parents.

When Maya Angelou said, "Do the best you can until you know better. Then when you know better, do better," she wasn't speaking to adoptive parents.[1] However, her often-quoted words ring true today for adoptive parents. Now that we know better, now that we've listened to research, adoptees, and birth parents, let's do better. We most certainly can do better. And if you're not sure what I'm talking about or how we can do better, my hope is that this book will serve as a guide.

This book will cover a variety of adoption topics, from honoring our children's ethnic heritage to everyday practicalities like haircare and meals and artifacts in the home. We'll talk about the importance of adoption allies and how to counter insensitive comments. And you'll read stories about our family, and you'll also find essays from adoptees throughout the book.

You saw "cross-cultural" in the subtitle of this book. Though we're talking about transracial and transcultural adoption, cross-cultural incorporates these two individual ideologies. I use cross-cultural because I'm not only speaking to transracial adoptive families, but I'm also talking to transcultural adoptive families as well.[2] If you're new to adoption, stick with it. I know it can take a little while to learn adoption jargon, but you soon will. I've included a list of explanations of adoption words at the end of the book to help those of you who are new to the adoption world.

IF YOU'RE A PROSPECTIVE ADOPTIVE PARENT...

Maybe you're reading this book as a prospective adoptive parent. There will be times when you feel uncomfortable and wonder, "Is she trying to talk me out of adoption?" I'm not. I don't want you to forsake adoption, but I do want you to pursue adoption in a way that honors the dignity of every person in the triad and in a way that reflects the very goodness of God.

And if honoring the dignity of each person in the adoption triad is difficult, I'm asking you to consider doing two things. First, take some time away to ask God to work on your heart and to sit and listen to adoptees, birth parents, adoption experts, and adoptive parents. Second, figure out how you can invest in your adoption community and support those who are working in family preservation.

If you're a two-parent family, this book is meant to be read together by the both of you! It is so important that both parents be on the same page when it comes to adoption—not only in your decision to adopt, but in how to respond to the many unique situations your family will walk through as a cross-cultural family. So consider reading this together and use the questions at the end of each chapter as a catalyst for conversation. And not only that, but if you have eager family members and friends who want to walk alongside your family, consider gifting them with a copy of this book so they can learn alongside you.

AND FOR NON-ADOPTIVE FAMILIES...

Maybe you're not reading this as a prospective adoptive parent, but as clergy, a family member, or friend who wants to support adoptive families or simply learn more. Welcome! I have written a chapter specifically with you in mind. I cannot tell you how happy I am that you're picking up these pages. One of the (many) difficult aspects in the adoption journey is educating the friends and family supporting us so that they can be safe spaces for our families. We need pastors and Sunday school teachers and friends who are literate in the adoption world. So thank you for taking the time to sit and learn about something that doesn't directly impact your immediate family. Thank you for entering into this space with us. "It takes a village to raise a child" is a common adage, but is especially significant in the adoption community. Adoptees and their families need allies. And as believers, we believe that the family of God should be one of the safest and best places for our children to thrive. Lord, let it be so.

CARING AS GOD CARES

From the beginning, I want to be clear about this: I fully believe that where there is heartache, devastation, and despair, the gospel speaks a true and better word. We serve a God who has promised to one day right every wrong and wipe every tear from our eyes. The grand narrative of Scripture points to a glorious redemption, and every day in between creation and Christ's second coming, He is still working for His glory and our good.

Adoption is something believers care about because God cares about it. Scripture tells us that God is in His holy place when He is being the Father of the fatherless and protector of widows (Ps. 68:5).

We care about the ethics of it, because God cares about the ethics of it (Deut. 10:18; Ps. 10:14).

He cares about the children, expectant moms, the single moms who decide to parent, the birth parents, the social workers serving tirelessly, and yes, the adoptive families. And as believers we have the opportunity to portray God's unconditional love and heart for justice here on earth, right now (James 1:27).

A FEW MORE PLANKS FOR YOUR JOURNEY

It needs to be said plainly, I do not speak for all members of the adoption triad. *I'm speaking as an adoptive parent to adoptive parents, potential adoptive parents, and people supporting cross-cultural adoptive families.* There are *many* adoptees and birth parents speaking out about their corner of the triad, and I think it is so incredibly important to listen to them, but I also think there needs to be some in-house conversation happening in our corner of the triad as well. It is not their job to educate us, but it is our responsibility to learn.

The goal of this book is to simply put another board in your bridge to creating a family where all members of the adoption triad are honored. As such, it must be stated that this is not an exhaustive, one-stop encyclopedia on all-things adoption. I'm not building the whole bridge with one book; I'm giving you a few planks to get you a little further along in your journey and, although I hope you find this resource incredibly helpful, I hope it's not the only resource you seek out!

And so now that you understand the purpose of this book, I want to let you in on a humble confession, dear reader. I am but a fellow journeyer, one who has not yet arrived but is still learning, repenting, and running after Jesus. Speaking of Jesus, you should know that if you're reading this and not a practicing Christian, you are more than welcome here. But please know that my faith informs so much of my life—well, all of it really—and this book is written from a Christian perspective. Still, my hope is that these practices and chapters are helpful to all cross-cultural adoptive parents. On that same note, many of the adoptees and sources who have contributed to this book hold to a diverse set of beliefs. Again, I believe that we can be united in pursuing healthy adoption practices while differing on other matters.

We have the opportunity through community development, orphan care and prevention, family preservation, and adoption to ensure that every child has a safe family to belong to. I pray that these upcoming pages will serve to that end. And, as the title of the book reminds us, it takes more than love.

QUESTIONS FOR REFLECTION

1. When it comes to transracial or transcultural adoption, what's one area you want to grow in?

2. Is there a specific topic that you're fearful or hesitant of talking about? Why do you think that is?

3. Do you tend to be a more optimistic person (everything is going to be *great*!) or a more pessimistic person (the world is falling apart!)? What impact do you think your tendency will have on the children you adopt into your home?

CHAPTER 2

Shedding the Savior Complex

When I was in seminary, I took my first mission trip to Kenya.

I had been on trips to Mexico and Brazil as a teenager, but this was my first trip to the continent of Africa. Our primary goal was to come alongside the local missionaries living there and to encourage their family, assist their local church and, since it was for graduate school, get credit for a class. It was an ethnomusicology course, so it was incredibly fascinating to study and learn how other cultures use music and, specifically, worship through song and dance.

At one of the church services in a smaller village, a child took a liking to me. She sat in my lap and wanted to be by my side all day. At some point, one of my classmates snapped a picture of us. Then later, throughout the week, we went to visit a school the missionaries were connected to. Again, with our cameras in tow, I came home with pictures of my White face in a sea of Black and Brown ones.

These were the days long before Instagram, but when I got home, what did I do? I did what every twentysomething did back in the early days of Facebook. I uploaded an entire album of photos from my trip, and I changed my profile pic. And what picture did I choose? Well, I chose the one of me holding that little girl. The comments from friends after they looked through my pictures were telling.

"Oh, I saw pictures from your trip! I'm so glad you got to go. And that little girl, is she an orphan?" "It's so good of you to go and serve! I'm sure it meant a lot to those poor people."

Keep in mind, this was a little girl I had met at a church. She was not an orphan. She had parents and a family and food in her home. She was a sister in Christ. She was Kenyan and she dressed like many in her village. She had a T-shirt on and a skirt with a vibrant Kenyan print. I was young and although the comments didn't sit well with me, I didn't have the language or wisdom to name what felt off.

First, I'm not going to pass the buck here. I was the one who made the mistake of showcasing my trip on social media in a way that elevated my "goodness" and "servant's heart" on the backs of a community that looks and lives differently than I do. Second, I unknowingly enjoyed playing the role of hero—or as some put it, I had a savior complex.

TO THE RESCUE

A savior complex is when Western people (often White) from wealthy countries go and volunteer or serve in poorer (often Black or Brown) countries in order to be a good person or hero.[1] Now, serving isn't bad in and of itself. For the Christian, we believe in a life of serving others. However, the savior complex distorts Christlike service by making the mission trip be about the volunteer. When you see photos of the trip, the narrative usually appears to be more of a humble brag about the volunteer rather than a photo journal of the work that's being done by local leaders or the work that the Lord is doing in a local community.

When we talk about serving "the least of these," we exacerbate the notion that people in poorer countries can't help themselves, so they need wealthy people to come over and help them help themselves. (One principle in the Helping Without Hurting series by Steve Corbett and Brian Fikkert, which I highly recommend, is to find out what the locals are already doing and ask how you can support them long-term, rather than swoop in to "fix" everything for them and then return home.) And somehow in the midst of sharing our story, we forget that we too are "the least of these." Jesus came down to earth because, well, none of us could save ourselves.

Now, when I went on my trip, I didn't have the attitude that I was coming to save the poor. I didn't adhere to the idea that I was better, or even that my culture was better than theirs. But still, I cringe at young Brittany in her twenties wanting to change the world and posting pictures of her travels. What was truly needed were fewer world-changers and more ordinary people who were both curious learners who loved God fiercely and were compassionate fellow journeyers.

To this day it's the same. We need people who want to learn about other cultures, participate in restorative work

We need people who want to learn about other cultures . . . and that goes for the adoption community too. Saviorism has crept its way into Christian adoption circles, and to be clear, there are no heroes in adoption.

within their own communities, and learn about restorative work from local community leaders all over the globe. We need more humility in our community development and mission work and significantly less exploitation. We need people serving and volunteering, but we don't need heroes. We need people who are captured so much by the glory of God that they don't seek out glory for themselves.

And that goes for the adoption community too. Saviorism has crept its way into Christian adoption circles, and to be clear, there are no heroes in adoption. And if there are, it definitely isn't the adoptive parents.

I can't tell you how many times I've been praised for adopting. In fact, the movie *Instant Family* has a scene where the foster parents talk about what would happen if they stopped the process. Things had gotten difficult and they were having a bit of a meltdown, and they joked about how people would stop thinking they were such amazing people. The movie brings the topic up in jest, but any person who has adopted or fostered knows this to be true and it's not a joke. I've been thanked in grocery stores, restaurants, airports, church—you name it!

It is a weird phenomenon that, quite frankly, is unhealthy for both the children hearing it *and* the adoptive parents receiving undue praise. The children might wonder, "What's so weird or bad about me that someone feels the need to praise my mom for being my parent?" and as a result have a decreased sense of self-worth and pride. And the parents can easily get an inflated sense of self and pride. Both are problematic.

Adoption is not a feel-good rescue story where parents are heroes and children are helpless victims. Instead, I think it's best to remove the lenses of rescue, helpless, hero, and victim and rather look at it from a more nuanced perspective. Adoption is loss and gain and trauma and family. It's complex. And all members of the triad *should* feel those tensions. No one member of the triad should be a hero, no singular member of the triad should be helpless, and no one should be a victim or villain. Those are not the roles we play. Rather, we stick to our roles of adoptive parent, birth parent/family, and adoptee. Those are the roles we have, and assigning others are unhelpful at best, and extremely harmful at worst.

Adoptee Melissa Guida-Richards wrote in *What White Parents Should Know about Transracial Adoption*, "You add in friends, family, and strangers all feeding into the narrative by calling adoptees lucky, by telling adoptive parents that they're angels, and by telling adoptees that they should be grateful. This narrative reinforces the idea that adoptive parents are saviors. . . . The savior narrative that my parents and many other adoptive or prospective adoptive parents are familiar with often emphasizes taking care of children by embracing them into the adoptive family—often without also adopting and embracing the child's birth culture, language, and first family."[2]

THE HANDS AND FEET OF JESUS IN COMMUNITY

Some of you might be wondering, "But Scripture tells us to care for the poor, the widows, and the orphans among us. We're supposed to help!" You're right. The Bible is clear on how God feels about the marginalized, the oppressed, the wounded. And even among Christians we can find those who are consumed with comfort, power, and success to the neglect of those whom God loves. Christians should always champion the flourishing of others. We should be unafraid to enter hard circumstances because we know that God has called us there. We should be about the flourishing of others and the welfare of our city (Jer. 29:7), because our flourishing should be connected to the flourishing of others.

And yet, we have to ensure that when we're living out our faith and being the hands and feet of Jesus, we're not centering the narrative around us. We live out our faith *in community* with the marginalized and the oppressed and the orphans and widows, rather than separated out as helpers or saviors. When it comes to transracial and/or transcultural adoption, the welfare of adoptees and birth families and single moms and expectant moms should be tied up, together, with our own family's flourishing.

Christians are people who value service, doing good, and loving others. So you might be wondering, "Okay, how do I balance living out my faith without it getting weird? What is it exactly that *should* separate Christian adoption from a savior mentality in adoption?" In my opinion it boils down to four things. It's your attitude, motive, posture, and impact, and we're going to walk through some questions to help you evaluate your own heart.

ATTITUDE, MOTIVE, POSTURE, AND IMPACT

Attitude

What is your attitude toward your child's first family, ethnic group, or local community?

Do you believe that your way of life is better than theirs? Do you think your culture, customs, food, and holidays are more important or more intelligent or more evolved than theirs? Is your overall attitude positive? Is it honest and fair? Or is it informed by stereotypes instead of research and factual information?

The answers to these questions won't tell you everything, but they're a good place to start. If you have a negative attitude toward your child's birth culture, there is a good chance you have a bit of a savior mentality. If this resonates with you, don't lose hope. Keep pressing in and remember what we've quoted: "Do the best you can until you know better. Then when you know better, do better."[3]

Motive

Have you thought, "Oh wow, people will think we're really great people"?

Do you think you are earning a better standing with God by adopting? Do you, in any way, think people looking at pictures of your cross-cultural adoptive family are going to assume you are just amazing people? Do you swell with pride when someone praises you for adopting?

Is your predominant motive for adoption to gain a baby for your family—or is it to provide a home so that every child has a safe and loving home? Is the goal of adoption to fill a void in *your* life—or is it to meet a need in *a child's* or a family's life?

These questions aren't exhaustive. But the overall question is, are you somehow twisting your motive for adoption in a way that serves or brings the focus back to you?

Posture

Your posture is the way you frame your adoption story. It's how you both verbally and non-verbally communicate your motives and your attitudes about adoption and your child's story. And it's also the trickiest to nail down. So rather than ask you a series of questions, I'll ask only a few. Is your posture one of pride or humility? Is your posture one of compassion for others or concern about your needs? Is it others-focused or self-centered?

Pride shines the light on you; humility avoids the limelight. (Now, also, beware of Christian false humility, which is another form of pride.) But if you adopt, this is one that we all need to be really careful with. Pride says, "Look at us, we're doing this really awesome thing." Humility says, "I believe that every child deserves a safe and loving home, *and* that families should have every chance of staying together." Pride says, "God adopted us as sons and daughters, so look at us, doing this admirable thing all on our own." Humility says, "We are called to reflect God's redemptive nature, so we do what we can, with what we have. And for every family that looks different."

Where there is compassion and care for others in your adoption story, there will be little room for exploiting their heartache for your virtue signaling gain. When there is great care for others, there is little room for you to care about yourself shining. When your posture is one of humility, it's okay to be called out and make mistakes because you're already well aware that you are flawed and in need of a great Savior (Jesus).

Impact

When confronted, I've heard adoptive parents say, "Well, I didn't mean to hurt you that way!" They use their good intentions as a defense mechanism to minimize the hurt and impact of their actions. This is why it's so important to wrestle with the question "What is my impact?" This question isn't just one that we ask ourselves, it's one that we ask others. We know that taking pictures of local children on mission trips is exploitative because we've listened and learned about the impact from local community members firsthand. As adoptive parents, we can examine adoption "best practices" and their long-term impact by listening to adult adoptees who are bravely sharing their stories. We look to adoptees and adoption experts who are performing actual research and publishing it in journals, books, podcasts, and yes, even social media (although that shouldn't be our primary source of education).

We examine our impact by not centering the results around our intention, but by centering how our actions and words impact our children.

The reality is, we're going to fail our children. But when we center the impact of our words and actions, instead of our good intentions, we develop a posture where grace and humility can grow. We're actually modeling the Golden Rule: "So in everything, do to others what you would have them do to you" (Matt. 7:12). We're doing to our children what we hope would be done to us if we were wounded by the actions of a loved one. We're modeling what it looks like to be human and flawed, and yet still motivated by love to pursue a healthy relationship full of grace and humility.

IF YOU'RE CARRYING A SAVIOR COMPLEX

What if at the end of reading all of this, you're realizing that yes, you do have a bit of a savior complex? What do you do with that?

Well, I want to say congratulations and I'm genuinely proud of you. Self-reflection and honest assessment got you here and that is a lot of hard work. Christians have gotten into the habit of forgetting that we all are broken people who make mistakes and are in need of grace. So recognizing this in yourself is a part of practicing true Christian faith. There is always room for fellow grace-seekers. But what's next?

First, I deeply believe this is a spiritual issue, so we start with prayer. Pray and ask God to convict you of the sins of self-elevation, pride, and saviorism. If you're already an adoptive parent, ask God to open your eyes to the ways this affects your parenting, your relationships with other members of the adoption triad, and those outside your adoption triad. Confess Jesus Christ as your one and only Savior, and repent of trying to take His place here on earth.

The second thing we do is repent. Repenting is the practice of confessing wrongdoing and then turning away from it. It is both verbal confession and then physically distancing ourselves from bad habits or wrongful thinking. This can take many forms, but it is an action that requires naming the sin and then running from it. If it is pride, it might mean you confess your pride and then ask your spouse, friends, or family to call you out on it when you talk about adoption in a prideful light. If it is a posture, you must confess it as wrong and then create a strategy—with the Lord's help and the wisdom of others—to work toward changing your posture.

And the last thing we do is restore. This is the active practice of righting the wrong. Where you've caused harm, you right the wrong. Where you've wounded others, you do whatever it takes to help facilitate healing. This can take multiple forms. If you have a teenage or adult child, this might mean you ask them what you need to do to right the wrong. If you have younger children, it means you start fighting against ethnocentrism and you start pursuing building a truly multicultural family where their racial identity can thrive. Restoration isn't a singular conversation, but a journey toward healing and redemption.

Other chapters in this book will help you build a safe family where adoptees can thrive, but this chapter—well, it's less about the actions and more about the heart. Let me encourage you to sit with some of the questions about your attitudes, motives, and posture and pray through which areas need some attention.

Remember, one of the greatest gifts we have in being a follower of Christ is that we don't have to cling to the pretense of perfection. No, because of Christ, we have the freedom to recognize that we are but mere humans, complex and imperfect, on a journey to being made more like Him. All believers should cling to that truth, but for adoptive parents, this is especially good news. We have no need for pretense, because we know that God is making all things new. We will make mistakes, but instead of digging our heels in the ground, we can raise our hands in the air in surrender: "Lord, help us do better."

QUESTIONS FOR REFLECTION

1. Was there ever a time in your life when you've witnessed (in someone else or yourself) an unhealthy savior mentality? What did it look like? What impact did it have on both the individual (with the savior mentality) and the community they were "helping"?

2. Which is more important, intent or impact? Why?

3. Of the four areas to examine—attitude, motive, posture, and impact—which one do you think you're most prone to exhibit a savior mentality in?

CHAPTER 3

Race-Conscious Parenting

I'm going to assume that you've picked up this book because you long to lovingly care for your child or your potential child. And if you didn't want to talk about or learn about race, ethnicity, and different cultures, you probably wouldn't be reading a book like this or considering cross-cultural adoption. So let's plunge right in.

In recent years, conversations on race have been politicized and polarized. Let's set aside what culture has said about race and racism and remember that the flourishing of every image bearer is something every Christian can be unabashedly for. My guess is that if you're here, you already acknowledge that racism exists. However, if you're a White adoptive parent or a prospective adoptive parent who doesn't think racism is a really big deal, I ask that you read this chapter with an open heart and mind. And if that is a task you can't do, I'm asking you to pause and reflect on why this is a sensitive issue for you.

I'm also asking you to consider not adopting a child of a different ethnicity or culture than you if you are uncomfortable having this conversation. That sounds extreme, but the more I listen to adoptees who were raised in color-blind homes where racism wasn't acknowledged, the more I believe that this is incredibly harmful to a child.

Before we dive into this chapter and begin this journey together, I'd like to—from the beginning—draw your attention to many phenomenal leaders writing about race and anti-racism and Christian unity. I'm forever grateful for brothers and sisters like Jemar Tisby, Latasha Morrison, Eric Mason, Derwin Gray, Eugene Cho, Trillia Newbell, Shai Linne, Francis Chan, Beverly Tatum, and many others who are doing great work, and much of what I've learned is attributed to sitting under their wisdom and leadership. I'm entering this chapter with great humility as I, a White woman, can only guide you on the things that I have learned from others. Entire books have been written on this topic and one chapter can't fully do it justice, but I hope and pray this chapter is simply a catalyst for further learning and growth. And I hope it is a testimony that God is for unity. If He has called you to adoption, He's calling you to work toward His redemptive design for unity, fairness, and diversity within your family and community.

IS RACISM REALLY STILL AN ISSUE?

I have memories of explicit racism occurring in my childhood. One day, my dad, a pastor, said that he had received a phone call from an interracial family traveling through our area and they wanted to know if their attending our church on Sunday would be a problem. I was naïve and young, so I asked, "Dad, why would anyone have to call and ask that? We're a church and the church is for all people—isn't it?"

He replied, "Yes, but there are some churches who actually *would* have a problem with that. Racism still exists today. And some churches in our area aren't exempt from it." My dad welcomed the couple and assured them that our church would be a safe place for them to worship, but the reality that an interracial family would call ahead to churches to make sure they would be welcome made an impact on me as one of my earliest memories of racism.

During my teenage years, I can remember hearing about a Biracial teenager at our local high school finding a noose in his locker, and I have memories of people talking about "those schools" in another county with a significant BIPOC population. I've had similar experiences as an adult too. Just last week I overheard someone make fun of a Hispanic family—and here's the kicker. These are people who boldly proclaimed, "Oh, I am not racist!"

The reality is, as a White person who was raised in White culture, I know that many of the people who have strong racial biases don't even know or recognize that they have them. But racism exists, and one of the greatest tools used to keep racism going is denial of its current existence. Since we all can agree that racism is bad, we can't imagine a world where racism exists in our own hearts.

The White little girl's mom yelled, "What did you do to her?" at my three-year-old, beautiful Black boy.

And yet it does.

I remember when one of my sons was just a toddler and he was in a play place at our family's restaurant. I was watching our kids when a little White girl walked in. My son, excited for another playmate, waved and smiled at her from five feet away, and she started screaming and crying and ran out of the play area. She ran to her mother and pointed at him. Catching what was going on, I quickly told my three-year-old, "Baby, when that little girl comes back in, I want you to give her some space. You've done nothing wrong, but go play with your sisters." Off he toddled, and a few minutes later the little girl came back. As soon as my son came down the slide, she started screaming and pointing at him. He wasn't anywhere near her, but her mom came in. Not knowing that I, a White woman, was a Black boy's mom, she yelled, "What did you do to her?" at my three-year-old, beautiful Black boy.

I stood up, physically placed myself between her and my son, and knelt down saying, "Go and play with your sisters, you haven't done anything wrong." And then I stood up, looked at her, and said, "He didn't do a thing other than smile and wave at her. He hasn't come near her, but every time your daughter comes in here, she points at him and screams." She still didn't realize that I was his mother (or that our family owned the restaurant she was dining in), and she persisted. "Oh, he definitely hurt her. She wouldn't act like that if not. He was being aggressive."

Now, calling Black boys "aggressive" is a racially triggered word and from that point on I knew, with certainty, that this woman was biased against the color of my son's skin.

"Ma'am, I've been in here the whole time. Your daughter is afraid of my son, but I can assure you it's not because he's done anything wrong." The little girl was afraid of him because she had absorbed the messages in picture books, shows, and most likely her own family that Black boys are dangerous; they're "aggressive" and to be feared. And yet, the idea that her small child was exhibiting racist tendencies didn't even cross that mom's mind. Her denial of racism and complete assertion that Black boys are aggressive made it impossible for her to see the truth.

Thankfully, an employee was also in the play area and she piped up as well. "Ma'am, we've both been in here the whole time and he did nothing wrong." The woman stomped out, dragging her daughter, while my son played, blissfully unaware. And after she left, I collapsed on the bench as tears welled up in my eyes. Our employee just patted me on the shoulder and said, "The world shouldn't be this way, but it is. Some folks are racist and just don't know it."

Having her name it was a relief to me, and yet the grief was heavy. My presence protected him on that day, but I knew that there was coming a day when my friendly, smart, Black son wouldn't always be protected by my presence. He would be labeled aggressive, and I wouldn't be there to defend him. Logically I had always known that, but that day my heart felt it acutely.

LET'S TALK ABOUT IT

I tell you these stories not to prove that racism exists, but because in every instance of racism mentioned above, most of the people who you would identify as racist would deny it. The churches in my hometown that wouldn't want an interracial couple to worship with them would boldly say, "We're not racist! We love all people. We just don't think the Bible condones such a thing and we want to keep our church pure." The parents of the kids who hung the noose in another child's locker would probably say, "They aren't racist! They're good kids, on the honor roll even! They just made a bad decision and were joking and took it too far like all kids do." And that mom in the play place most definitely was in denial that her White daughter was terrified of the only Black child in the play area, despite the fact that he was smiling and exhibiting a friendly, welcoming demeanor. And she labeled him aggressive without witnessing any of his behavior.

Denial is what keeps ethnocentrism, color blindness, and racism alive. So, before we work through some of these, we have to take a good long look at denial. Before we get too judgmental of others, it's important that we wrestle with what's in our own heart too, mine included.

I've had thoughts and made assumptions about people based on stereotypes. But the best way forward isn't denial, it's confession and repentance. It's taking those thoughts captive and giving them to the

Lord. "God, forgive me and help me love and see people like You love and see them."

When I am talking with someone who proclaims color blindness or says they don't have a racist bone in their body, I've learned that those proclamations are giant red flags because they've not done the work to examine what our culture has proclaimed for so many years. For example, my children's storybook Bibles, until we intentionally looked for others, were full of pictures of White Jesus and White children. If we believe that we're impenetrable to the messages that these images and others are saying about the presence (or lack thereof) of people of color, we are deceiving ourselves. If we don't do the work to wrestle with the messages we've been taught or if we deny that they ever existed, we make room for racial biases to thrive and grow unchecked.

My children's storybook Bibles were full of pictures of White Jesus and White children. If we believe that we're impenetrable to the messages that these images and others are saying about the presence (or lack thereof) of people of color, we are deceiving ourselves.

If you're preparing to be an adoptive parent or if you are supporting an adoptive family, my biggest piece of advice is to intentionally take some time to pray, reflect, and wrestle with the racial biases that exist in your own heart. And if you truly don't believe that you have any, I still recommend taking the time to work through an anti-racism guide just as a refresher and for further learning (my guess is that once you dive in, you might be surprised at what you find).

Be the Bridge, an organization created by Latasha Morrison, has multiple workbooks and guides that can walk you through race, including one specifically designed for transracial adoption. Cam

Lee Small is a licensed counselor and a Korean American transracial adoptee who created an *Adoption and Race eCourse* that you can purchase and work through at your own pace. These are just a couple of examples, but many churches and Christian organizations have gospel-centered resources that walk you through God's heart for redemption and reconciliation.

The point is, racism exists in this world and racial bias has the potential to exist in each of us. The best thing you can do is to take the time to listen and learn from experts, and then grow and change in the grace of Jesus Christ. As I've mentioned before, as Christians we have an advantage knowing that we're all sinners in great need of a Savior. None of us is above having discriminatory thoughts or stereotyping. And so we go to the throne of grace asking God to help us love and see all people like He sees them.

TAKING IDENTITY NEEDS SERIOUSLY

In *Why Are All the Black Kids Sitting Together in the Cafeteria?* Dr. Beverly Tatum says, "The importance of the parents' role in helping children make sense of the social comparisons they are making, as well as other race-related experiences they are having, cannot be overemphasized."[1] This is true for all parents of minorities, but adoption adds an additional layer. She goes on to specifically mention transracial adoptive parents:[2]

> Race-conscious parents who openly discuss racism, who seek to create a multiracial community of friends and family (perhaps adopting more than one child of color so there will be siblings with a shared experience), who seek out racially mixed schools, who, in short, take seriously the identity needs of their adopted children of color and try to provide for those needs, increase the likelihood that

their adopted children of color will grow to adulthood feeling good about themselves and their adoptive parents.[3]

I love the line "take seriously the identity needs of their adopted children." If I could leave you with an encouragement from this chapter, it would be to take seriously the identity needs of your children. In order to do so, we must address two ideas that you will encounter as a transracial adoptive family: ethnocentrism and color blindness . . . two things that every adoptive family needs to check at the door.

Ethnocentrism

I recently participated in a training session on transracial adoption where the moderator, who was an adult transracial adoptee from China, shared a story about her upbringing.[4] She talked about how, as a child, she remembered her parents and their friends talking about China as politically and socially inferior. She can recall them talking about "communist China" and how whenever her birth country was discussed—outside of her adoption—it always held negative connotations. Here was a little girl, who was Chinese, being raised in an all-White family and the only thing she can remember being taught about her home country was that they were communists.

Ethnocentrism, says Dr. Brian Howell, is "the use of one's own culture to measure another's, putting one's own culture (*ethno*) at the center (*centrism*) of interpretation, typically devaluing and invariably mischaracterizing the other culture."[5] Howell explains that ethnocentrism is normal and inevitable because all humans are socialized to look at their way of life, their family structures, and their culture as the standard for the norm. However, he argues, "it is important to become increasingly aware of our own ethnocentrism so we can recognize how our own culture shapes our interpretations and interactions with others."[6]

We see the same mentality in adoption when adoptive parents

or their community elevate their culture over the culture of their child's birth country. This happens when we focus on the positive our culture offers and neglect to acknowledge the negative, and then focus on the bad things in another culture and neglect to acknowledge the good.

For example, if an ethnocentric American couple adopts a child from China, they might only discuss "communist China" and the one-child policy, while neglecting to celebrate China's beautiful family-centered culture, their many technological accomplishments, and the diverse and stunning geography throughout the country. They might boast of America's freedoms while neglecting to discuss the racism that has unfortunately been part of our culture. They might brag about our freedom of religion but omit how women and minorities weren't allowed to vote for much of our country's history.

Many people naturally take great pride in the country they call home, but our pride in our birth country doesn't have to diminish the pride others have in theirs. If anything, we can serve as bridges for our children to embrace both their birth culture and the culture of their current home country by ensuring that both are honored in our homes. They shouldn't have to choose one or the other, as they are physical embodiments of both. They might be Ethiopian Americans or Asian Australians or Haitian Canadians, and it is a gift to be able to celebrate both aspects of their ethnic and adoptive heritages equally.

Color Blindness

Color blindness is "rooted in the belief that racial group membership and race-based differences should not be taken into account when decisions are made, impressions are formed, and behaviors are enacted. The logic underlying the belief that color blindness can prevent prejudice and discrimination is straightforward: If people or institutions do not even notice race, then they cannot act in a racially biased manner."[7] This is an issue that has long plagued adoptive communities, and many transracial adoptees are speaking out about the harm of being raised in a family that ignores their ethnicity.

Color-blind parenting denies the realities that your children will face when they are no longer under the protection of your presence.

Writer, author, and transracial adoptee Rebecca Carroll was asked by television show host Trevor Noah, "Should White people be adopting Black children?" She said she was very much loved by her parents and that she believes transracial adoption can work. However, she warned, "If White parents adopt Black children and they don't make very conscious decisions about incorporating, including, immersing, valuing Blackness, then it's deeply problematic. It's not just one doll; it's not just one poster; it's not just one mentor. It's really an immersion process that has to happen . . . and so should White parents adopt Black children? If they are prepared to raise Black children into Black adults, then yes."[8]

Carroll is talking only about White and Black cultures, but truly this could be applied to any ethnicity. Color-blind parenting does not equip your child to live in America as an Asian American, Haitian American, Indian American, and so on. Color-blind parenting denies the realities that your children will face when they are no longer under the protection of your presence.

There are many people who are critical of transracial adoption right now. However, in my opinion, it seems like they aren't critical of adopting cross-culturally. They're critical of people adopting and then ignoring how important racial identity is to transracial and transcultural adoptees. They're critical, and rightly so, of a color-blind approach to adoption. Sure, there are some who are adamantly opposed to transracial adoption, but what I hear more often than not is a plea for adoptive parents to forsake a color-blind mentality.

If you've taken the time to read or listen to transracial adoptees' stories of being raised in color-blind homes—and I believe that by reading this book, you're already taking these steps—you know how important this is. Many adoptees, who love their adoptive families, are sharing just how isolating, confusing, and difficult it is to navigate their racial identities. They have graciously and bravely shared how a color-blind mentality that has infiltrated the adoption world has done significant damage to their mental, emotional, and spiritual health. And so we, adoptive parents and their supporting community, would be remiss if we don't heed their words of wisdom and handle their stories with care.

We talked about denial earlier, but color blindness is the cousin of denial when it comes to racism. It's one of denial's many fruits. One of the things about color blindness that I've learned over the years is that many White people use color blindness as an expression of hope for our future and disdain for explicitly racist acts. Over coffee with friends I've heard some form of the following: "I don't see color. I don't get it. I just want everyone to be treated equally." Many color-blind people have some of the best intentions. They truly want to live in a world where ethnicity doesn't have a negative impact on a person, without understanding the negative impact of a color-blind mentality. But having a color-blind attitude doesn't actually help get us to that world, because our present world very much so sees color. Sociologists and racism experts alike have expressed fear over the refusal to recognize that pretending to not see race actually allows people to ignore discrimination.[9]

But more than that, as Christians, we know that unity of the body doesn't mean we have to pretend that ethnicities don't exist. Latasha Morrison says it this way: "In the love of the family of God, we must become color brave, color caring, color honoring, and not color blind. We have to recognize the image of God in one another."[10]

I love how the grand narrative of Scripture acknowledges and celebrates our various ethnicities, and at the end of it all Scripture tells us that in heaven—embodied in our skin, language, and culture—we will be praising our glorious God:

> After this I looked, and there before me was a great multitude that no one could count, from *every nation, tribe, people and language*, standing before the throne and before the Lamb. They were wearing white robes and were holding palm branches in their hands. And they cried out in a loud voice: "Salvation belongs to our God, who sits on the throne, and to the Lamb." All the angels were standing around the throne and around the elders and the four living creatures. They fell down on their faces before the throne and worshiped God, saying: "Amen! Praise and glory and wisdom and thanks and honor and power and strength be to our God for ever and ever. Amen!" (Rev. 7:9–12)

Every time I read that passage I smile and tears spring to my eyes! What a vision! But not only that, we're asked to model that vision here and now, on earth as it is in heaven. All throughout Scripture we're told that it is good for brothers and sisters to live in unity (Ps. 133:1; Rom. 12:16), called to work toward restoration and unity (2 Cor. 13:11; Col. 3:14), to be of one body and one mind (Rom. 12:4–5; Phil. 2:2). We are told that the good news of Jesus is for both the Jew and the Gentile (Rom. 1:16; Gal. 3:28). And we have been given the great commission and greatest commandments, which call us to love and baptize people of every nation and tongue. Our God calls us to unity within diversity, not unity through cultural assimilation and uniformity.

> *"Diversity in and of itself also is a good thing, and unfortunately differences aren't always celebrated in others."*

And so those of us with diverse families live these truths out by rejecting a color-blind mentality and embracing God's good design in diversity. Christian author and speaker Trillia Newbell says this about color blindness:

> Unless you are truly color blind, you see color. And this is a good thing! I understand that such statements are said with good intentions, but what might be more accurate is to say that you don't immediately equate characteristics and stereotypes to a color. That's obviously also a good thing. But diversity in and of itself also is a good thing, and unfortunately differences aren't always celebrated in others.[11]

As adoptive parents, whether it's through transracial or transcultural adoption (or both!), it is vital that we see our children's ethnicities because they are God-ordained, beautiful expressions from a good and holy Creator. Ignoring them or pretending they don't exist prohibits you from celebrating how your unique child reflects *imago Dei*. As Christians, we believe that all people are made in the very image of God, and that truth is special, because out of all the things that God created, humans are the only ones stamped, imprinted with God Almighty's likeness.

And this has implications for our parenting! As Newbell stated above, diversity is a good thing, and for the adoptive family it is an opportunity to celebrate and reflect God's good design in our homes. So instead of having a color-blind mentality, we see our children's varying ethnicities as opportunities to celebrate God's creativity and sovereignty. And although in the past some of us have gotten this wrong, I'm so grateful that God is moving in the adoption community and He is calling us to do better.

IN YOUR TOOLBOX

This chapter has a lot of information, and the last thing I want is for you to read it and walk away confused at what to do with it all. I want to leave you with some action steps that will help you in your journey. This list isn't exhaustive, but it's a great start to get you going:

Read and listen to anti-racist books, articles, and podcasts by BIPOC. I love to read, and books were my introduction to anti-racist work. They introduced me to ideas and concepts and stories I needed before engaging deeply on the topic with people in person. Books are helpful because they keep you from placing the responsibility of education solely on the shoulders of minorities without doing your own work. Over the last few years there have been many books released by both Christians and non-Christians on the work of anti-racism and racial reconciliation. Read widely on this topic, and also take advantage of the many online classes as well as church-hosted webinars. If you adopt transracially or transculturally, you will be wise to invest in cultural training and anti-racism training.

Different isn't weird, and it doesn't equal better or worse. One thing we practice in our family when we encounter another cultural norm (even when we're just visiting other family and friends) is saying, "It's not weird. It's not better or worse, it's just different." We want to give our children language to encounter something different without elevating their way of doing life.

Words count. The ways we talk about our children's birth countries and first families matter. Do you only talk about the negative things you see? Or have you taken the time to learn about their country's beauty and cultural wins? Spend an evening

> *Our goal isn't to sever their relationship with their first culture; it's to hold space for them to be able to build a bridge to it, in whatever ways they're most comfortable one day.*

researching fun facts about your child's ethnic heritage. Learn about the political structures, the country's famous athletes/authors/poets/musicians/celebrities. Learn to cook one of their cultural meals. Find ways to celebrate and talk about their culture in an honest and beautiful way. But whatever you do, don't trash talk your child's home country, culture, or first family. Remember, our goal isn't to sever their relationship with their first culture; it's to hold space for them to be able to build a bridge to it, in whatever ways they're most comfortable one day.

Recognize the flaws of your culture. Sometimes it is easier to turn a blind eye to our own sins and focus on the sins of others. Scripture talks about this in Matthew 7:3: "Why do you look at the speck of sawdust in your brother's eye and pay no attention to the plank in your own eye?" When you find yourself having a critical heart toward another culture, consider taking a moment to intentionally reflect on ways your culture gets it wrong. And then work to help right the wrong in the places God has you.

Take an implicit bias test. Harvard University's Project Implicit has an online test that examines your implicit biases.[12] I highly recommend taking one of these exams and learning more about implicit biases.

Intentionally celebrate other cultures. We talk about this in other chapters, but it is critical that you intentionally celebrate and incorporate your child's first culture in your home as a family. Read books, attend festivals, cook cultural meals, honor holidays, join a local community group . . . whatever else you can think of. Incorporating your child's first culture in your home is a must for the adoptive family!

Travel and plan a trip. If you've adopted a child transculturally, this is a very important thing to plan for. International travel is expensive (as is adoption), but it's important to plan for if you've adopted internationally. Your child needs to have the opportunity to visit their birth country. Some people call these "heritage trips," but whatever you call it, it needs to be incorporated into your family planning. It feels privileged to suggest that you should do it as often as you can afford, but doing this with your child is such a gift not only to them, but to you. Planning a heritage trip where your child gets to learn about their culture, see the unique beauty of their country, and learn about their lives before adoption is a healthy step in them owning their origin story and developing a healthy cultural identity.

Be curious. My friend Alicia is quite possibly one of the best question-askers I know. She is genuinely curious about the world, God's Word, and the people around her. I've seen her listen to someone else's experiences and then ask questions to learn more about it. Rather than looking at life only through her lens, she tries her best to understand the viewpoints of others.

When fighting against ethnocentrism, ask good questions of others and then genuinely listen. Be curious about their experiences, their culture, the way they see the world. Allow your curiosity to lead to learning.

Be explicitly anti-racist. Once you've read the books and listened to anti-racism experts, it's time to start taking action. Do you lovingly correct your friends and family when they say or do something racist? Are you a part of discipling a new generation that understands the doctrine of *imago Dei*? Does your church use a multicultural Sunday school curriculum—or are the graphics predominantly White? What about your school system? How are Black and Brown women treated in the organizations you serve in? Are they in leadership? Are they valued? What are the demographics of your local prison?

Don't do this alone or start a new ministry. Look around in your community and partner with organizations and churches that are already doing gospel-centered anti-racism work!

If you are adopting cross-culturally, it is incredibly important to be able to identify ethnocentrism, color blindness, and racial bias in your family, community, and culture and to combat this with a more inclusive approach where your child can be safe and develop a healthy racial identity. Be sure to spend time with your spouse and/or community working through the questions below.

QUESTIONS FOR REFLECTION

1. What is one new thing you thought about or learned from this chapter?

2. Reflect on your life, your values, and upbringing. Can you think of an area in your life where ethnocentrism exists? (For me, it's being time-oriented. When I travel internationally I have to remember that the way I approach time isn't better, it's simply different.)

3. Do you, or did you ever, have a color-blind mentality? What's one way you can grow in that area?

4. Out of all the tools listed in the last section, what is one step you can do right away? Take a few moments to map out a plan of action of things you can do with your family and/or friends.

ADOPTEE VOICE

by Kennedy, Black Transracial Adoptee

The Journey Continues

I am Black.

I am a woman.

I am transracially adopted.

I have known these facts from the beginning. But I am just learning what these mean to me. It is hard to be viewed as an adoption success story when at its foundation there is loss. I recently heard that as an adoptee you can't talk about adoption/your life story without hurting the other two members of the adoption triad. As someone who in the last few years was educated on the adoption triad, this statement simultaneously rattled and comforted me. I realized that I've had a textbook "good life"—great education, fulfilling career path, and a family that does not negate the loss that I experienced from infancy. But I have not allowed myself to examine or feel that loss because that requires hurting another member of the triad. And yet, ignoring that loss is not honoring the beautiful triad that I am a part of.

I feel like there has not been a large enough platform to hear from transracial adoptees unless it speaks to the gratitude or "privilege" of being adopted. I really hated the expectation that I should feel gratefulness and that this feeling should be the primary one.

It takes an emotionally healthy and secure parent to begin a conversation highlighting the grief and loss that took place and will continue to show up throughout an adoptee's life. This made me realize why I've shied away from talking about my own story. I never wanted to say anything that would hurt my family, but I also wanted to respect the choice my first mom made. However, in doing that I never allowed myself to grieve. No matter the story, adoption is trauma, complex, and layered.

To safely process the loss, there would need to be freedom to not worry about how parents would respond or internalize it. As an adoptee, I

50

often worried about how my response or emotions would negatively affect a parent. I can only imagine how freeing it would have been to hear, "I'd love to create space for you to talk about the grief and loss you may be feeling with adoption. If that space is with me, please know that I will put your emotions first and those emotions are important. If not with me, how can I help you find a safe adult to talk through that with?" How powerful to hear! You don't have to worry about hurting either part of the triad; you just need to feel your own feelings as an adoptee. I think allowing myself to process and grieve would help connect me to my identity.

One area that I've recently allowed myself to grieve is the loss of not growing up in Black culture or a Black community. While being Black is not a monolith, the culture runs deep. It was really hard for me to balance being Black and Christian. I was in spaces that elevated white voices, theology, worship, and teaching. As if to say, this white way is the right way. I desperately wanted to connect with a Black faith community.

My first experience of that was during college (side bar: I would not recommend this). There was a community feel among Black students because we did not feel accepted or represented through the student body. Our faith was too demonstrative, our voices too loud, the collective too joyful within a predominantly White culture. And during these pivotal years, this was the space I was craving but didn't know how to "belong." It caused me to question and doubt the ways I was showing up and I struggled with imposter syndrome.

I wish I had had consistent connections with Black communities growing up to help me begin identifying who I am as a Black woman. Exposure to Black culture in real life and through TV shows or movies would have helped introduce me to the richness and variety of being Black. I wish I had statements like "Because I am Black on purpose" and that "My Blackness is a reflection of Creator God" to help me fight those insecurities and imposter feelings.

I am so thankful for all the resources to connect to Black communities. I am thankful for the Black church from which such history, beauty, safety, and knowledge about God are experienced. I am thankful for the multiethnic churches that are elevating Black voices and creating communities. As a transracial adoptee (TRA), it would have been amazing to grow up in one of those spaces.

As I reflect, it was the Christian spaces that felt the most isolating, specifically my church and conservative Christian college. I remember my mother advocating when we needed to find a new church that the church and pastor would be accepting of our transracial family, that the pastor would be supportive on all levels including if his child were to date or marry one of us. And although I am thankful that she understood a piece of what it meant to advocate for your Black child in a white space, it highlights how far some churches have to go. It once was this proud memory of my mom, but now it is discouraging thinking about how that was my formative faith environment.

I am still identifying what it means for me to be a TRA Black woman, but I am thankful for a family who always made me feel loved, a life partner who has helped connect me to Black culture, children who are reminding me to fully show up in my Blackness, and a supportive community that is celebrating, learning, lamenting, and honoring this history.

The journey continues!

CHAPTER 4

More Than Haircare

When we were in the adoption process for the first time, we brought dinner over to some church friends' house. Chris, prior to going into the ministry, was a barber and we were asking him for good barber recommendations in our area. While he was sharing he quickly said, "You do know that in Black culture you don't cut your child's hair their first year of life, right?"

Ben and I quickly looked at each other. "I didn't know that, did you?"

Chris and his wife laughed. "Yeah, you can't do that. But when the time comes, we'll point you in the right direction."

It was the first of many times we relied on friends for guidance on beauty, haircare, and traditions for our children. Over the years, we had to learn quickly that the beauty standards for our White family are significantly different from other cultures. And we didn't want to simply be a White cultured family with different skin tones; we wanted to be a multicultural family where each of our children's ethnicity and beauty standards were respected and practiced.

In her memoir, Biracial transracial adoptee Rebecca Carroll wrote about her experience having to learn about haircare on her own because her White adoptive parents had not done so. She talked about how she had no clue how to part her hair or massage oil on her scalp, and how it took meeting and becoming friends with other Black women who took the time to do it for her.

Before you think this is an outlier, it's not. As you listen to adult adoptees of all ethnicities you'll hear similar stories of having their hair and skin washed too much or too little. You'll hear about how adoptees were raised celebrating their parents' standards of beauty, without the tools to embrace their own culture's beauty traditions. You'll hear about how they heard their parents and other adults in their lives degrade other ethnicities' aesthetics and talk poorly about the shape of their eyes, their skin, their height, and so on.

I follow a variety of adoptive families online, and one of my favorites is a Black Haitian mom who is married to a White American man. They have both biological and adopted children, and one of their little girls is White. The other day she was talking about the importance of hair care for her White adopted daughter and my heart almost exploded. Too often in the United States, we assume that transracial adoptees are always people of color. But more and more, as adoption systems become more equitable, BIPOC parents are adopting—and adopting White, Black, Indigenous, Hispanic, Asian, European, African, and American children.

And it is incredibly important that if you have a transracial or transcultural adoptee of any ethnicity you learn about their specific beauty needs.

One of my favorite stories to tell is the day I met a Black foster mom at Pullen Park in Raleigh, North Carolina. It was a hot and humid day in Raleigh, which isn't unusual for summers there. My son was only a few months old, and the twins were three. Now, our girls' hair was fine when they were little. I'd pull their blonde and wispy hair up into a sweaty, tiny ponytail with a bow, but half of it would escape the tie because that's just what their baby hair did.

We had just gotten off of the train that carries happy toddlers around the park, when one of the twins pulled her bow out and I was putting it back. I was wearing my son in a wrap, and a nice woman came up to me and asked, "Is he yours?" Distracted by a squirmy three-year-old, I didn't initially notice the ethnicity of the baby that she was wearing, nor did I see the White toddler girl in her stroller. I smiled quickly and said, "Yes!" And then she said, "I'm a foster mom and I was wondering if I could ask you a few questions about dealing with fine blonde hair that won't stay in place and gets so tangled." I looked at her quickly, and then laughed and almost hugged her due to the sheer joy of meeting another mom parenting transracially and said, "Well, I'm definitely no beautician, but I would love to swap advice!"

It takes courage to make a new friend and ask for help when it comes to learning how to properly care for your children's beauty needs.

I told her some tricks we used on our girls' hair and skin. And she gave me some tips on what to do with my son's hair and skin. I was just a few months into being an adoptive parent, but I love how God orchestrated the paths of these two moms to cross so we could identify with each other and our transracial parenting journeys. And I learned something from her that day that I'm not sure I would have otherwise. It takes courage to make a new friend and ask for help when it comes to learning how to properly care for your children's beauty needs.

The truth is, if you're a transracial adoptive parent you're not going to automatically know all the beauty standards and cultural norms of your child. You weren't raised with that specific set of beauty standards, so you shouldn't be embarrassed that you don't know about them. And sometimes with adoption, you might not have time to learn about your child's cultural beauty practices until you're placed with a child.

For example, we received a phone call the day our first son was born telling us that he would be placed in our home. We didn't have weeks or months of preparation. And with our second son, we will have to learn about his ethnicity from a DNA test given later in life due to conflicting information we've received along his adoption journey. However, if you're adopting internationally, you might have months or even years to prepare! The point is, you can't know what you don't know, but once you do know it's your job to put in the work and start learning.

And in this day and age, we have so many resources accessible. Whatever ethnicity you are and whatever ethnicity your child is, there's a tutorial on the internet to help you navigate learning how to properly care for your child's hair and skin. There are adult adoptees hosting workshops and licensed beauticians making videos on social media. The internet has taken away every excuse, but I must say that although I use a quick google search often, my favorite way of learning is from friends in our community. I am waiting for the day when one of our sons grows up and asks me, "Mom, why in the world did you do that?" And my response can be, "I don't know, I'm White so I asked Ms. Fabiola and Mr. Donté and that was their advice, so call them up and ask them!" We have a plethora of resources available at our fingertips with the internet, but what we need more of is real and lasting relationships.

BEAUTY AND RACIAL IDENTITY

In *Outsiders Within: Writing on Transracial Adoption*, Jeni C. Wright shares in an essay titled "Love Is Color-Blind: Reflections of a Mixed Girl."

Memory #1

I'm nine years old and have just finished taking [a shower]. I catch a glimpse of myself in the foggy medicine cabinet mirror. . . . I move closer, wiping the steam away with the edge of my towel, and start to weep.

My face looks like it belongs in the National Geographic movie on Africa we watched in social studies last week, the one Mrs. Dunbar had to turn off in the middle—she hadn't known there would be bare-breasted women in it. The boys I play kickball with at recess didn't talk about anything else all week.

I lean over the sink so my nose is almost touching the glass and mouth to the ugly girl staring back, *you look like an ugly African bush girl*, over and over until my breath clouds over my face. I start to write "jungle bunny" in the steam but I am crying too hard to finish. Why hadn't anyone told me I was so ugly? I don't even look like a real girl.

Opening the medicine cabinet, I reach past the Q-tips for my father's little black comb. My quest to comb my curly short afro flat to my scalp keeps me in the bathroom for close to an hour. It feels like forever, especially because in the end I fail. That night I write in my diary until my fingers ache as bad as my scalp. The first sentence of my entry is, "It's a good thing I'm smart because no one is ever going to marry me."[1]

When I first read the essay (and this is just a portion of it), I held my breath because I could feel her turmoil and anger. Her disgust with her aesthetic was tied directly to her embodiment of a cultural heritage being lived out in a predominantly White community with Eurocentric beauty standards. Her adoptive parents, regardless of intentions, had neglected to teach her that she was beautifully made in the image of God. Her skin, her hair, her intellect, her voice—all of it—reflected a God who made her. It reminded me that the work of representation is more than just a few books on the shelves and ensuring that your kid goes to the right type of barber.

This issue is more than just hair and skin care. It's more than just using the right products and staying up-to-date on styles (although, let it be said plainly: please do that too). It's a step in helping our children build a healthy racial identity. It's setting them up for success as adults. It's helping them incorporate their cultural standards for beauty in our homes and families while not making them feel "other." It's journeying with them and not making them navigate their racial identity and beauty standards alone. It's allowing them to explore and be creative with their "look" and helping them connect to their racial identity as they grow older. It's living out the truth that every nation, every tribe, and every tongue reflect the very image of God and so we welcome and honor that in our homes. It's not holding our ethnicity's standard of beauty as the norm, but making space where all can grow and thrive.

WORDS THAT CREATE SPACE FOR BEAUTY TO GROW

When our older son was two or three, we would practice catechisms with him.

"Who made you?" I would ask.

"God," his tiny little toddler voice would reply.

"Why did God make you and all things?"

"For His glory!" and he'd raise his hands in the air and point to the sky.

We'd also quiz him on Black history. "Who is the first African American president?" and he would enunciate "Barack Obama" with his tiny little toddler voice ("Ca-rock Oh-bom-ee" was how he said it the first time—my apologies, Mr. President).

In addition to teaching our children truths about God, we want to teach them about their cultural history and their worth and value as members of a specific ethnicity. So around the age we start cat-echizing our children in the faith, we also start racial identity affirma-tions. We start small with one phrase, and then build on it over time. At bedtime, you'll hear us talking about God and reading books with our kids, but then you'll also hear us say to our son, "Okay, who are you?"

This isn't some weird self-help mantra. It's a phrase that has cre-ated space for him to start developing a healthy racial identity. Some-times he says, "I'm a smart Black man who loves God." Sometimes we add things to the end of that sentence depending on the circum-stances of the day. For example, "I'm a kind Black man who loves God and I'm a good friend." Or "I'm a strong Black man who loves God and I can do anything I put my mind to."

But the point is, we want him to be able to recognize the beauty, dignity, and strength of his ethnic heritage from an early age in order to fight the lies that a racialized society will attempt to place on his skin.

I do the same thing when it comes to my daughters and beauty. Early on I would tell my girls how smart and capable they are. I'd commend them for their bravery and kindness. I'd also affirm their beauty as I know the world we live in will try to make claims about what beauty is and isn't. So in our house, we start these affirmations early and we get specific.

We talk about skin, bodies, strength, intellect, and eyes to give them the words to name the beauty that comes with their specific ethnicity that God has given them.

"I love how God made your arms so strong!" when I see them carrying a heavy box. "I love how God gave you beautiful eyes. Isn't it cool how God makes all of us different?" "I love to hear you laugh. It's like beautiful music to my ears." "Wow, you finished that book! You worked so hard and I'm so proud of you!" We do this with all our kids, but we are especially intentional to create space for our transracially adopted children to see and name their cultural beauty in our home.

When we're getting ready for the day, I stand behind our older son while I put product in his hair and I tell him how much I love his beautiful Black curly hair, and isn't it cool how his hair is a lot like Mr. Thomas's? And how his skin is dark and beautiful like Mr. Donté's? And we tell our younger son that his beautiful brown eyes just sparkle and how he has his birth mama's smile. We talk about skin, bodies, strength, intellect, and eyes, using our hands to help and not hurt, and we do all this not just to build confidence in our children, but to give them the words—the tools—to name the beauty that comes with their specific ethnicity that God has given them.

And not only that, I make a point to affirm the beauty in other people in our home out loud to my children and invite them to join me. "I love how kind Ms. Emma is, and doesn't she have such a beautiful smile and laugh? She is so creative and organized in ways that mommy isn't! Isn't it great how God makes each of us unique? Isn't Ms. Makayla so beautiful? I love her brown skin and her beautiful hair. And she is so smart and such a hard worker too. I'm so thankful for her friendship and what I learn from her." These are all phrases that my kids have heard me say when leaving the presence of dear friends.

We'll talk about different tiers of representation in chapter 6, but for now know that it can be an amazing thing to watch your children affirm the beauty and dignity of people who are from different ethnic backgrounds, various heights, skills, and sizes. I love how we'll get in the car after leaving our friends' house and our girls will say, "Sara just got her hair done; didn't it look beautiful?"

If you haven't been doing this, starting now might feel forced if you have older children. But there is no time like the present to start incorporating this in some form or fashion that serves your unique family. And if you're a prospective adoptive parent, this is something you'll want to start doing from the beginning so it becomes a natural practice in your home.

We're going to be talking about how our words have a profound impact on our children in chapter 10 (specifically when we're asked questions about adoption). But on that same note, words left unsaid can also wound them in profound ways. Aside from the normal affirmations that every child needs to hear, the transracial and/or transcultural adoptee needs to hear words affirming the beauty of their ethnic identity. Children need to know that their parents are safe spaces to talk about differing beauty standards, what their friends said about their hair, or any feelings of otherness they will have. So from an early age, we start with affirmations, but we grow as our kids grow. If we leave these specific words unsaid, we are allowing the world to shape our child's thinking on their culture's beauty.

Whether your child is Asian, Hispanic, Black, Biracial, Native American, Indian, White, Middle Eastern, Polynesian (or any ethnicity that is other than your biological family), you will need to instill in them a sense of worth and identity rooted in Christ, but also an identity that affirms and defends their ethnicity's unique beauty.[2] Adoptee Bonita Croyle suggests creating a "shared commitment and shared language"[3] as a family so our elementary-aged children understand what racial slurs are and how to spot them on the playground. They also know what to do if they think someone is being bullied or left out because of racism. Our small children know that they are beautiful and have permission to tell people to not touch their hair or their bodies. They know how to educate their peers by saying, "My skin (or eyes or hair or height or body) isn't weird just because it's different from yours. It's beautiful and it's the way God made me."

And we do this in a consistent, fun, yet educational way from the time they are little. This is why we do affirmations. This is why we teach our kids when they're toddlers, "Your hair is beautiful. Your skin is fabulous. Your eyes are amazing. God made you just the way you are. And if anyone else tries to tell you otherwise, what do you say?" We wanted to gift them with the tools to combat attacks on their God-given beauty, because we already know the lies that this world will try to sell them. In our family, we want to do everything within our power to equip them to fight lies with life-giving, gospel truth.

Scripture says, "The tongue has the power of life and death" (Prov. 18:21).

Our words have power. We shape the culture of our homes with our words. We shape the spaces where our children learn about their identity, their beauty, and confidence. And as parents, we are on a mission to create life-giving space with our words where our children know, without a shadow of a doubt, two things: (1) They are beautiful just the way they are, because (2) they are made in the very image of a good and creative God. We fight racial and gendered stereotypes and lies that this world will tell them about their beauty, not by sticking our heads in the sand and holding children to our cultural beauty standards, but by creating space with our words and actions where their cultural beauty practices are affirmed, celebrated, and welcomed in our homes.

QUESTIONS FOR REFLECTION

1. Have you ever experienced the pressure of maintaining a cultural beauty norm? How did that make you feel? How did you respond?

2. Identify one of your culture's beauty standards.

3. Now, identify what your culture says about beauty in other cultures.

4. Write out an affirmation that you believe would benefit the child/children in your family.

ADOPTEE VOICE

by Elle, Black Transracial Adoptee

Good Hair

I was a sophomore in college when someone first told me I had "good hair."

I was shocked, because up until this time all I had ever thought about my hair was the complete opposite. Growing up the Black daughter of White parents, in a time before YouTube tutorials, I struggled to like anything about my hair. Weekly or nighttime hair sessions were often marked with anxiety, frustration, and tears. Each Black woman has her own "hair journey," in which she learns to understand the ins and outs of caring for and maintaining a healthy head of hair. Navigating these challenges in a household where your hair is so different from those around you is an added challenge.

As a young girl, I was often subjected to teasing because my hair often looked poorly styled or unkempt. I longed for a hairstyle that would help me blend in with my family, believing it would help people see that I really did belong. I wanted to feel beautiful without feeling a need to be altered. My mother would occasionally take me to a neighbor's house or a Black hairstylist and beg them to help make my hair more "manageable." With my hair in braids I seemed to stand out in my majority white spaces, and hear statements such as, "Oh wow, how does your hair do that?" Or "That is so interesting, are you able to wash that?" All while they touched my hair as though I were an exhibit in an art show.

My mother would often complain about the amount of time and work it would take to wash and style my thick coarse hair. There were many combs broken and many tears shed as I complained about the long hours spent sitting on the floor, as my mother tried to re-create the hairstyles she saw on other Black girls my age. I did not want to be the Black child with the braids, while my friends were able to wear their silky locks out with never anything more than a headband to keep their bangs out of their eyes. My mother eventually decided to have my hair chemically straightened, believing this would be the magic that would finally tame my unruly locks. She was ignorant of the continuous maintenance that was necessary to keep my tresses straight and healthy and this eventually led to damaged hair and a tortured scalp.

By the time I had entered college, I had spent countless hours on styling and trying different products to re-create hair styles that my White family and friends were able to wear. My sense of confidence and acceptance correlated with how I thought my hair looked to others. When my Black roommate said to me, "You have such beautiful hair. Why don't you ever wear it natural?" I began to realize that I felt unable to fully embrace or even understand how to style my natural curl pattern because for most of my life I was trying to fight against it.

There is no denying the emotional connection our hair plays in our self-identity. I am now a married mother with two daughters of my own, and though I still blow dry and straighten my hair, I have also embraced wearing my hair in its natural state. It took having a daughter of my own for me to finally feel comfortable being "me" and to love and accept my hair in all its versatility. I want my daughters to feel accepted and celebrated for the things that not only make them like others, but also the attributes that make them unique. My girls will have their own hair journeys and I pray that I instill in them the confidence and care I needed along with my own.

Part 2

_____

ADOPTION IS COMPLEX

CHAPTER 5

Offering Our Presence in the Hard

Let's begin this chapter with a fictional scenario:

Esther and Mei have been college roommates for two years, and over the last few months Mei has started wrestling with her identity as a transracial adoptee.

One day in their dorm, Mei confides in her friend. "I am so glad my parents are my parents, but I really wish that I had parents who looked like me and understood my ethnicity from lived experience, not just secondhand information. I don't know, it just makes me sad sometimes."

Esther squirms a little, uncomfortable with the conversation, and says, "Well, things seemed to have turned out fine for you. God always uses all things for our good and His glory. Obviously, this was

His plan all along to have you in this specific home, so I would just trust that this plan was for your good."

$$\Longleftrightarrow$$

"God always uses all things for our good and His glory" is an absolute truth that Christians hold. I want to be clear that I affirm this 100 percent. And yet, it is spiritual malpractice to use a truth to diminish the reality or hardship of someone suffering. It should not be used as an action step to bypass, in this case, an adoptee's normal and healthy wrestling with loss and racial identity.

"Spiritual bypassing" is a term psychologists use for something that can surface in Christian circles under the guise of what may seem to be spiritual truth. In an article for *Relevant* magazine, Alison Cook writes, "The term is tossed around a lot these days, and it's important to understand it. Spiritual bypassing simply means that you use spiritual concepts, platitudes, or activities to 'bypass' or avoid dealing with your true feelings, especially the hard ones like anger, grief, fear, loneliness, envy, and shame."[1]

One of the main aspects of spiritual bypassing in any given situation is that we use the good parts of our stories to ignore the hard parts. Rather than making space for both the good and the bad to coexist together, we bypass the hard and pretend that the end justifies the means. This goes for adoption.

When an adoptee expresses curiosity, grief, anger, sadness, or uncertainty about the hard parts of their story, it is spiritual bypassing to push them to gratitude. Pointing to what they gained without acknowledging and wrestling with what they lost is bypassing the trauma, the means, that got them there. Cook says it this way: "Instead of seeking to understand our emotions, we ask God to 'remove them' or 'work a miracle in our life.' Instead of letting our pain or anger lead us to healthier boundaries with others, we bury these emotions in the name of 'love' or 'sacrifice.'"[2] Her article includes a helpful chart on the difference between emotional health and bypassing emotions.[3]

Reacting to hard things in this way is not uncommon, but is it biblical? Consider the many psalms of lament. Also remember the story of the death of Jesus' friend Lazarus, and how He reacted: "Jesus wept" (John 11:35).

The danger is that trauma and hurt are simply ignored or minimized rather than wrestled with, accepted, and then processed to develop a healthy response.

Listen, if you're a Christian, we proclaim and believe that all things work together for the good of those who love God. But you wouldn't use those words to stop the grief of a sobbing mother who just lost her child. You wouldn't tell her, "Well, you should just be grateful for the time you had with your child. God has a plan for this and for you, so you should just trust Him." That's insensitive at best and in the end doesn't glorify God or benefit the grieving one!

And yet we do something similar to adoptees.

The danger here is that trauma and hurt are simply ignored or minimized rather than wrestled with, accepted, and then processed to develop a healthy response. Children, in turn, internalize this grief and shame and learn that their parents are not safe places to truly wrestle with difficult topics related to their adoption.

And make no mistake, spiritual bypassing can be done with or without a faith practice to guide you. But for many people of faith, we use a redemptive narrative we see in Scripture to help push along the process. We use absolute truth to squash any personal narrative that involves pain, rather than allowing that truth to make space for the hard chapters on our journeys.

The truth is, no one gets a pass when it comes to pain in this life. And bypassing it is like taking Tylenol to quiet the symptoms without actually addressing what's causing the pain. The pain will flare back up when the medicine wears off, and the longer you put off dealing with the issue, the worse it can become.

For Christian adoptive parents we must learn to "rejoice with those who rejoice; mourn with those who mourn" (Rom. 12:15). We must hold space for the hard parts of our children's stories and be ready to not bypass them quickly, but to stay in the trenches for as long as it takes. We use Scripture and truth as anchors, but we don't use them as band-aids. After all, the absolute truths we hold to in Scripture are more powerful than any healing a band-aid can offer.

The Lord is with us—not just at the end when things have resolved—but smack dab in the messy middle. This is an absolute truth we hold on to. It doesn't diminish any pain we or our children experience, but rather trusts that His presence is big enough to sustain it. It is an anchor to ground you, and a light on the path before you. *His presence doesn't mean you get to skip over the pain, the trauma, and the heartache, but it does mean that you're not alone in it.*

Bypassing our emotions negates that truth of God's presence that is central to our Christian faith. And although it might temporarily ease the pain, it will only cause additional heartache to whatever wound you're trying to avoid.

WHAT'S NEXT?

So what's next? How do we avoid spiritually bypassing our children's pain? There are three simple practices that will help set up a home where pain, specifically related to cross-cultural adoption, is dealt with in a healthy manner.

Find an adoption-informed counselor early on

Awhile back, we started hosting a Be the Bridge group in our home.[4] One night, during a session on forgiveness, I shared something I learned from a counselor. One of the group members expressed that he was grateful and surprised that I would acknowledge that I had gone to counseling. He, too, went to a counselor and felt like it was something that some people just didn't talk about. Despite all the strides we've made, there still seems to be a stigma in regard to counseling.

I want you to lean in close, because I'm about to give you some advice and say some strong words, but I need you to know that it's all in love: If you have a pulse and are breathing, you could benefit from some counseling.

Counseling isn't for the weak. It's for the wise.

That's it. That's the hard thing I'm going to tell you.

Some of you are breathing a sigh of relief because you already know that, but to some others of you, that sentence stirred up a defensive response. "I'm fine, I don't need counseling, and neither do my kids."

To those of you who have the latter posture, please, hear me out.

We all have experienced difficult things of all sorts. Life can be utterly brutal, and having a counselor to help guide you through the troubles that life can bring is nothing to be ashamed of. If anything, it's the opposite! It is wise to seek good counsel when you're hurting. Wisdom is what enables you to allow someone into the hard parts of your story to help you see things you couldn't so that you can eventually heal.

Counseling isn't for the weak. It's for the wise. And from my personal experience, a counselor offers objective and unbiased wisdom in helping you process whatever's going on, and then they help you develop a plan to take the next step forward in life. It's not a quick

If you are an adoptive parent, you need to find an adoption-informed counselor for your whole family, but especially for your children.

fix. It's not some magical, fluffy hour where your therapist or counselor hands you the keys to life and happiness. It's hard work, sometimes painful, but also an incredibly helpful tool. And wise people know when they need help obtaining tools they can't get on their own.

If you get nothing else from this book, I want you to take this one thing seriously. If you are an adoptive parent, you need to find an adoption-informed counselor for your whole family, but especially for your children. To be specific, you need a trauma-informed *and* adoption-informed counselor. Many adoption agencies can connect you to post-placement resources, but if your agency doesn't, don't let that stop you! There are plenty of counselors available for online video sessions, and a quick google search in your area or surrounding area can give you a good idea where to start.[5] And if finances are holding you back, I want to say two things. First, there is a myth that counseling is for the financially stable and able, but there are many adoption agencies that offer free counseling services and support groups to first families, adoptees, and adoptive families. Also, many nonprofits and churches offer affordable counseling services to adoptive families.

However, I also want to say this. Just like you save money for the cost of adoption, you should consider adding the cost of counseling services to your financial planning (just like you consider the cost of adding another dependent to your health insurance). There is too much at stake to just wing it. Did you know that adopted children are more likely to wrestle with depression and commit suicide than a non-adopted child?[6] Did you know that transracially adopted children tend to lack a strong racial identity?[7] There is too much on the line for your children in developing a healthy racial identity, learning how to attach, and overcoming neglect and abuse that not all, but some, adoptees have faced. And hear me out. Adoption—even at infancy—carries its own type of trauma that needs to be addressed head on.

Because I run in adoptive circles, I know what some of you are thinking. "Brittany, my child is fine. She's happy, she's doing well in school, and she has friends. I don't want to stir the pot." I hear you, but let me ask you: Are you listening to adult adoptees, many of whom are now using their time and experiences to help other adoptees wrestle with the hardship of adoption? Are you reading adoption-informed books and articles and magazines, many of which agree that children need to be able to talk about their adoption openly and have access to adults with whom they can safely process?

> *Many adoptees have been frank about not knowing how to talk about their adoption as they were growing up.*

Many adoptees have been frank about not knowing how to talk about their adoption as they were growing up, let alone issues like racism and developing a healthy racial identity, and they didn't know that they were allowed to explore these complex issues. A counselor can help you make your family a safe place for adoptees to wrestle with these complex issues so they don't feel isolated later in life.

I am an advocate for counseling in all areas of life. It is healthy to have a trusted professional who can help you process hard things, work toward goals, and give you an outside professional perspective, regardless of whether you're an adoptive family or not. I hope and pray that the stigma associated with counseling continues to decrease as we see its great benefits. However, if you're a transracial and/or transcultural adoptive family, your family must make mental and emotional health a priority. Denial is just another form of bypassing and counseling is one of the tools that can help you heal rather than ignore.

So, if you take nothing else from this book, please find a counselor who can help guide you to create an environment in your home where you can address the unique issues that your child has faced and will continue to face as a transracial adoptee.

Don't romanticize adoption

If you look on social media, depending on your corner of the triad, you might see a different set of hashtags. On the adoptive parent side, you might see #adoptionrocks and #adoptionisbeautiful, and on the adoptee side you might see #adoptionistrauma.

Here's the thing. Both sets of hashtags are true. If a child who lives in an orphanage gains a safe and loving family—this a beautiful thing. It's also traumatic to have a child lose their biological family and their culture, and then to be placed in a family who doesn't look like them. Both hashtags are technically true in this instance. But one perspective without the other offers only a piece of the puzzle.

In order to not bypass the tough parts of the story, it's important that we don't romanticize adoption. We cannot ignore the hard parts and only focus on the good ones. We cannot tell our children a romanticized narrative that neglects the hard parts of their stories, because eventually, one day, the hard parts will catch up with them.

Recently I was listening to a podcast with adult adoptees when one of them said that for the first two decades of her life she never really thought about the hardship of being adopted, but when she had a child of her own it triggered a deep grief inside her.[8] Prior to having a child, she wore the identity of a "successful adoptee" like a badge. But becoming a mother triggered many questions and eventually was the catalyst for her to figure out where she came from and to pursue connecting with her biological family. And it wasn't until her third decade of life when she really started to develop a healthy, holistic identity as an adoptee.

In another adoptee-centered podcast, Angela Tucker interviewed

Kristen, a transracial and transcultural adoptee from Paraguay. In the interview, Kristen said, in reference to her parents, "to talk about adoption is to hurt someone."[9] She went to South America as an adult and it was a profound experience for her as a transcultural adoptee, but she couldn't bring herself to talk about the trip in that way with her adoptive parents. And she was adamant that her parents were absolutely lovely and amazing, and they had never done anything to signal that they wouldn't welcome the conversation. But they hadn't done anything in her childhood to signal that they *would* welcome it either. As a result, the conversation felt out of place now.

Her parents had never done anything to signal that they wouldn't welcome the conversation about adoption. But they hadn't done anything in her childhood to signal that they would welcome it either.

This should never be the case.

If we romanticize adoption to the point where we neglect to have the hard conversations with our children while they're in our care, we are creating uncertainty in our adult children's lives when they are ready to discuss the hard parts of their story. Toward the end of the podcast Kristen said that she wished her parents had initiated conversations when she was growing up so she could talk freely about it now.

Every story is different and every adoptee is different. However, every adoptive family should be the same in their support of children wrestling with the hard parts of their story from childhood on. Our job as parents shouldn't be to give our children rose-colored glasses to view their adoption, but instead it's to help them see it clearly for what it is and then to give them the tools and support to tend to their specific needs. One way we can do this is to talk about adoption, and to talk about it often.

Talk about adoption, and talk about it often

When I was a pre-teen, I had a lot of "female problems." Medically speaking, I was diagnosed with Polycystic Ovarian Syndrome, and I was told that it was unlikely for me to be able to birth children without fertility assistance (the joke's on them seeing as I had surprise biological twins).

I remember sitting in that doctor's office after an internal ultrasound when my mom asked, "What does this mean for her future? Will she be able to have kids?" I don't remember what exactly the doctor said, but I do remember watching my mom's demeanor sink. I could tell she was devastated. I, however, was unfazed. I was young and never had been the type who dreamed about a wedding and babies, so that situation seemed so far off to me that it didn't apply. Later, when my husband and I were talking about having children, the gravity of the situation was heavier, but because it was something that I grew up talking about and knowing, it wasn't a traumatic blow.

The earlier you start talking about adoption, the better. The more you talk to your child about their story, the good parts and the hard parts, the more opportunities you have to teach them to own all aspects of their story.

And yet, I have watched friends receive the same diagnosis later in adulthood and it is jarring. Their hopes and dreams for having a family biologically were crushed, and the hardship that they walked through was different from mine, even if we had the same diagnosis. The difference? I had years of knowing my diagnosis. I had time to process and accept it while in the safety of a loving family. I had plenty of conversations with doctors, read books on the subject, and had gotten comfortable with the reality I was given. So, when my relationship with Ben got serious, it wasn't uncomfortable for me to own my story and say,

"There is a good chance I won't be able to conceive children without fertility treatments and I don't want to travel that road. I've made my peace with that, but I want you to be able to make your peace with that too. And if you can't, that's okay too."

Spoiler alert: He made his peace with it.

Obviously, the analogy isn't perfect. But the earlier you start talking about adoption, the better. The more you talk to your child about their story, the good parts *and* the hard parts, the more opportunities you have to teach them to own all aspects of their story. Of course, you need to do this in an age-appropriate way (which is why I am so passionate about having a trauma-informed counselor), but if you are going to be a cross-cultural adoptive family, you are going to have to frequently talk about adoption, loss, racism, forever family, birth family, unconditional love, and many more adoption-related themes. And the earlier you start the better. You can't stop or bypass trauma, but you can prepare your children from an early age to process, grieve, and come to terms with their losses.

It doesn't have to be perfect, but normalizing talking about adoption early on opens the door for children to talk about their feelings and questions later in life. Ask them questions like, "Do you have any questions about your adoption/birth family/origin story/culture/racism? How does _____ make you feel?" If you have pictures of your children before they joined your family, or of their biological family (or any piece of their personal history, for that matter), make sure they have access to it in age-appropriate ways. These can also be great catalysts for conversations. Some friends make books for their kids, so that at an early age they can flip through their pictures and keepsakes to develop a healthy narrative of knowing where they came from. There are many resources out there that have age-appropriate suggestions on how to talk to your children, but I've included two in the notes as a starting place for you.[10] But I also want to share what has worked for us.

In our family, we have a healthy open adoption with two of our children's first families. Although there is still more research to be done, much of what's been written points to the many benefits of open adoption for adoptees (strengthened sense of identity, healthy attachment to adoptive parents, and decreased sense of abandonment by first family).[11] So when one of our sons was a toddler, we had a cork board hanging in his room with pinned pictures all over it. Some of the pictures are from our family vacations, others are of family members and close friends. And some are pictures of him with his biological family from our visits. Every so often at night before bed, I would hold him in my arms and we'd go and look at the pictures. We'd point to one picture, and then I would point to the pictures of his biological family, and I'd ask him, "Who is this?" We had done the ritual so often that he knew all their names. And then I'd say, "This is your biological family. They love you very much and your birth mama is beautiful and strong and she chose our family for you. And isn't it amazing how your skin matches her skin? And you have her smile too?!" When he was a toddler, I didn't go into all the answers to *why* she chose our family or what led her to adoption. But around the age of five, I started introducing some of those to him as well.[12]

THE GIFT OF PRESENCE

During our second adoption, I had the privilege of getting to know our son's birth mother extremely well during her pregnancy. She met our children and spent lots of time with our family.[13] During a medical emergency while she was pregnant, I had the honor of staying with her in the hospital. I rubbed her feet, fed her ice cubes, helped her get to the restroom. I fretted over her pain and advocated for her to be heard when it seemed that her medical team wasn't listening to her.

I didn't recognize it then, but our bond went beyond the adoption triad we were planning on forming. I loved her for simply being her. And when the time came for the birth of our son, watching her walk through pain and grief and sorrow was one of the hardest things I've ever done. Once again, we found our-selves in a hospital room, and I cared for her as she and I cared for our son, feeding him bottles and getting her ice cubes and her favorite Starbucks drinks. Smiling while she was awake; crying and praying over her at night.

And now, even as I write these words, I'm feeling teary, because the love that we hold for our children's first families is just that intense. It is a deep love that has been tested. It's not some fairy-tale love that came easily, but it's a love that has been through many trials and heartaches.

Again, depending on the type of adoption you have, this might not be applicable, wise, or even possible! Some adoptions have minimal information. Some adoptions are completely closed.

Show your child that you acknowledge the gaps in their story and are willing to support them in discovering the truth about their origin. Affirm having negative emotions about loss and trauma, while also offering your presence as a support throughout the journey.

However, it's important to share what you do know without creating a narrative with falsehoods in it. For example, if you don't know anything about the biological parents, you shouldn't create a narrative that makes the child feel good about them if it's not factual. It's okay to not have all the answers. "I don't know and I'm really sad that I don't have that information, but I will work with you to find out everything we can about that," is a powerful statement. It shows your child that you acknowledge the gaps in their story and that you are willing to support them in discovering the truth about their origin. It also affirms having negative emotions about loss and trauma, while offering your presence as a support throughout the journey.

When you make space for the good and bad to coexist from the beginning, it is easier to continue the process throughout their lives. And if your child is older and you haven't really started talking about their adoption or their ethnicity, there is no time like the present. It's never too late to acknowledge that you've made a mistake (even if unintentionally) and you want to create a safe and loving relationship where difficult conversations and your child's thoughts, feelings, and questions in regard to adoption are validated and welcomed.

Most people don't enjoy discomfort and try to avoid it at all cost. But if we choose to enter into the world of adoption, we must intentionally choose to not bypass the discomfort our children will face, but instead choose to wrestle with hard things together, as a family. Perhaps the greatest gift we can give our children is our presence while they're in the beginning and middle parts of their story, rather than point them to the happy ending.

QUESTIONS FOR REFLECTION

1. Has there ever been a time when you've been on the receiving end of a bypassing-your-emotions-with-spiritual-platitudes type of messaging? How did it make you feel?

2. How do you hold on to theological truths, without using them to emotionally manipulate someone in their time of grief?

3. What are some practices you can develop in your family in order to foster emotionally healthy responses versus bypassing honest emotions in your home? You might want to refer to the chart in *Relevant* cited in this chapter's note 3.

ADOPTEE VOICE

by MJ, Foster-to-Adopt Adoptee

What My Mom Did Right

I am an African American adoptee, originally from the northeast, and I spent the first years of my life in several different foster homes and was adopted at the age of six along with one older sister. My birth parents were substance abusers, and they weren't able to care for me and my eleven siblings. I had an open adoption, so I was able to keep in touch with my biological family, and I even got to see them from time to time. It was a blessing, but it was also very confusing. Having to split my time between my adopted family and my biological family was so hard. I had two sets of parents, many siblings, and a few siblings who were old enough to be my parents.

After I was adopted, my mom made the decision to allow my sister and me to have contact with our birth grandma. My grandma had a huge part in my adoption. I spent the first five months of my life in my birth mom's care. She was a substance user, and one day she went out and left my sisters and me alone for a few days, until we were found by one of our neighbors. Two of my sisters were placed with my grandma, and one of my older sisters and I were placed in foster care together. My birth mom lost her parental rights during that time, and she was placed in prison. When my adoptive mom decided to adopt us, my grandma asked if she could have a relationship with my sister and me. My mom agreed and promised her that she could be in our life because she agreed that it would be helpful for us to get a chance to know our birth family. I was the youngest and I had so many birth siblings, and she would jokingly say, "I want you guys to know your family members because I don't want you to end up marrying one of them." I had biweekly visits with my birth family before I was adopted, and after I was adopted my mom agreed to still take us to see her. My grandma loved us, and at the time she was caring for two of my sisters, so I was able to see them during our visits.

My mom and my birth grandma had a great relationship. My mom would often write or call her to give her an update on my life, and my visits with my grandma were so sweet. She would, of course, spoil me like any grandparent, and she was there for me with whatever I needed. She tried to answer any questions I would have about our family and the situation I was in, but she also would encourage me to not repeat any of our conversations or share anything negative that happened at her home with my mom. I hated this and I always shared things with my mom because there were things that happened to us or things that were said that weren't quite right, and my truth-telling heart couldn't handle the secrecy of it all. My mom always responded in a nice way and tried to explain things to me, but she never kept me from my grandma. During these visits my birth mom would sometimes stop by. Because she was a substance abuser, my grandma wouldn't allow her inside of her home, especially if my sister and I were there. She always wanted to keep us safe. My birth mom wasn't a pleasant person to be around when she was under the influence of drugs, and one of the conditions of my grandma's visitation rights was that my birth mom wasn't allowed near us without having my grandma or my social worker there. When she would visit she would have to come to the outside window to say hello and my grandma would give her some food.

We moved to a state in the South a few years after I was adopted. I remembered being sad that I would never see my birth family again, and sadly I did not see them again until the day before my eighteenth birthday. Even though I no longer lived in the same state as my birth family, my mom made me call my grandma throughout the year to thank her for my gifts, to wish her a happy birthday, or to check in on the family. Every birthday and Christmas my grandma would send us a box of goodies or something small to let us know that she loved us still, and even though I had been adopted, she still was in my life. My mom made that promise to my grandma and she kept her promise.

When I became an adult, I remember my mom telling me that it was now up to me to decide if I wanted to have a relationship with my birth family. She said, "When you were younger, I made sure you called her, but now it's up to you." Because I had built a relationship with my grandma, I couldn't imagine life without her. I called her all the time until she passed away. She loved hearing about my travels and all of my achievements. She was proud of me. My mom still brings up my grandma and we will talk about all of the memories with her and how much she loved me. I am so thankful that my mom allowed me to have a relationship with her. I am named after my grandma and I am thankful to have known her and to carry her name.

CHAPTER 6

Representation Matters

I was on a podcast a few years ago when the hosts asked me questions from their listeners about transracial adoption.[1] This came from an adoptive parent: "How can I give a heritage that is not my own? Where does a parent start, and what framework can they follow, to ensure a child has all they need in knowing their ethnic identity?"

When I first heard the question my heart sank a little because I understood the issue those parents were facing. After all, what parent doesn't want to be able to give their kid everything they could possibly need to thrive? And I resonated deeply because when we first adopted transracially, the weight of ensuring that our sweet baby boy would grow into a well-adapted adult with a healthy ethnic identity would keep me up at night. I would rock, and worry, and pray, like most mothers do about one thing or another. But this thing felt heavy, and I felt alone.

My husband, Ben, and I started listening to podcasts and read books by transracial adoptees, and my heart sank even more because so much of the narrative focused on the many mistakes adoptive parents made. I'm so grateful for the bravery and strength that many TRAs (as transracial adoptees refer to themselves) showed as they shared their experiences in order to prevent future adoptees from walking down similar hard roads, but I also found myself struggling. I didn't want to make the same mistakes, but also, I recognized that most parents don't intend to screw up their kids. It's typically our blind spots that can do the most damage, so I kept listening and reading and praying that I would know better so I could do better.

I had listened to many adult adoptees retell stories from their childhood on how they had never been around people who looked like them until adulthood, and how that negatively impacted their ethnic identity and emotional/mental health. Like most moms, we want the world for our children. If there's a way to equip our kids to succeed, we'll fight tooth and nail to make it happen. And the reality that many of these adoptees' parents were ill-equipped or chose to not engage in the hard parts of their stories broke my heart.

You cannot give your child their ethnic heritage, but you can be a bridge, a connector, for your children to have access to others who can show them the way.

And so at night, I would rock and pray, and then during the day Ben and I were committed to learning more—to not look away from pain, but to press in. And what I realized in those sleepless nights, while cuddling my baby with his beautiful dark skin snuggled in my pale white arms, was that we did not alone have the capacity to give him his Black heritage. My blind spot was believing that with enough books and knowledge and classes, I'd be able to fill that void. But we are a White woman and a White man, and there was no way we could teach our son to be a Black man in America. And that's true for all transracial or transcultural adoptive parents. We cannot give our kids a cultural heritage that isn't our own.

Before you panic, hear me out. If left alone, Ben and I would fail miserably at teaching our son about his ethnicity because, although books and media are helpful, they aren't substitutes for the incarnational presence of people. We can give our son many things, but we cannot give our son his ethnic heritage. Neither Ben nor I can serve as a racial mirror for him. And although this grieved me deeply (and to this day it still grieves me that I can't do this for him), I have learned that instead, I can serve as a bridge builder.[2] My husband and I can build a bridge so that while he's living at home, he can always have access to his ethnic culture and a map to developing a healthy ethnic identity. And when he's on his own, as a grown adult, he'll be able to put more boards in his bridge and continue his own journey of racial identity.

The question of "how to give your child a healthy ethnic identity" is what still keeps me up at night. So whenever I'm asked, "How can I give a heritage that is not my own?" I always answer it the same way: You cannot. It's a hard pill to swallow as a parent, but it's something that we must embrace in order to be able to move forward. It's one of the first steps in simultaneously holding both the hard and the good that surround adoption. The beauty and the brokenness. The trauma and the growth. Always both/and, rarely either/or.

You cannot give your child their ethnic heritage, but you *can* be a bridge, a connector, for your children to have access to others who can show them the way.

WINDOWS AND MIRRORS

"Representation matters" is a popular phrase right now that I fully support. It is a critical concept in the life of all children (white, black, brown, male, or female). As I write this book, I am in the final journey of finishing up my doctoral degree. My dissertation's focus is on racial representation in Christian children's literature. And if I've learned but one thing throughout the journey, it's that words have power, and meaning changes with time, but the idea of equal representation for our children is a timeless concept that should be embraced during all seasons.

Children need windows to see into other cultures to build curiosity and empathy, and they need mirrors to see their own culture represented in a story.

If you'll do me the honor of letting me share some of my doctoral work, I want to give you a very brief lesson on racial representation in children's literature and why it is essential. And although we're talking about books in this section, this concept can be applied just about anywhere—the leaders we listen to, the shows we watch, the organizations we support, the folks at our table— but I want to lay the groundwork now for how it will look discussed at the end of the chapter.

Dr. Rudine Bishop is well-known in the education world for naming the "windows and mirrors" concept in literature. Books and pictures and stories can serve as mirrors, a reflection of a person's identity within a society; and they can also serve as windows, glimpses into other peoples' culture and places in society.

So when we say "representation matters" when it comes to the books we read, we're saying that children need windows to see into other cultures to build curiosity and empathy, and they need mirrors to see their own culture represented in a story.[3] When there's an imbalance, perhaps too many mirrors and too few windows, a child can become more ethnocentric and narcissistic. According to Bishop, if children only see "reflections of themselves, they will grow up with an exaggerated sense of their own importance and value in the world—a dangerous ethnocentrism."[4]

On the flip side, having too few mirrors is also problematic. Dr. Bishop states, "When children cannot find themselves reflected in the books they read, or when the images they see are distorted, negative, or laughable, they learn a powerful lesson about how they are devalued in the society of which they are a part."[5] When books serve as mirrors, children "can recognize characters like themselves, building a sense of self-esteem and significance."[6]

Now consider the transracial adoptee, a minority within a family that doesn't look like them. Think about the books on the shelves of that home, the movies and television shows watched, the church and school that they attend. Think about their pastors, school counselors, doctors, and coaches. Having a surplus of windows into another culture and a deficit of mirrors can have a negative impact on racial identity and growth.

So what do we do? How do we make sure that "representation matters" isn't merely a slogan in our homes, but rather a lifestyle we live out?

THREE TIERS OF REPRESENTATION

Over the years, I've broken down the concept of racial representation into three specific tiers for the cross-cultural adoptive family. These three concepts are meant to work together, but they're also listed in the order of easiest to more difficult. Oftentimes, adoptive families start with the first tier and then grow into tiers two and three. However, I want to stress that if you are a cross-cultural adoptive family, you should be incorporating all three tiers into your family's life.

If you're strong in tier one, but haven't started doing work in tiers two and three, you might not be ready to be an adoptive family. However, if you already have adopted, don't waste time on feelings of guilt.

There is no time like the present to start making some significant changes. Remember Maya Angelou's words: "Do the best you can until you know better. Then when you know better, do better." We're not going to waste precious time beating ourselves up; instead, we're going to keep learning and then doing better for the sake of our kids.

And on a personal note, many people find, regardless of their family makeup, that pursuing an intentionally diverse life is not only fulfilling, but models a "thy kingdom come" mindset, the traditional words from the Lord's Prayer. Heaven is a glorious place where every nation and every tongue will be praising God together. When we intentionally choose lives that have both windows into other cultures and mirrors for ourselves and our children, we model "on earth as it is in heaven" in our homes. So, if by chance you're a grandparent, a friend, or just a monocultural family that wants to fight against ethnocentrism in society, this list is a fantastic place to start.

Tier 1: Representation in artifacts and culture inside your home

One of the easiest ways to start living out your belief that racial representation matters is to ensure that the artifacts in your home reflect that value.

Consider: Does the artwork in your home reflect the cultures of everyone living in it? Where is the artwork and decor in your home purchased from? This is something we have been working on the last few years. During the holidays, we wanted to include our children's ethnic heritage in the Christmas decorations. Since my husband and I are White, we wanted to fight against having predominantly Anglo Christmas decor, so we have invested in ornaments, nativities, and artwork that represent everyone in our family. During the rest of the year, the quotes we have hung up and the books on our shelves reflect the people living in our home.

Are the adult books you read written and illustrated by diverse voices? Or are the only diverse books segregated out for the children?

It's important that this is a shared value for your whole family, not just the children who joined your family through adoption. What about the music you play inside your home? The television shows and movies you watch? What types of cookbooks and recipes do you use?

What about your children's books? Do you have kids' books that provide both windows and mirrors for your children to see themselves and learn about other cultures? And to take this one step further, do your children have books where the main character, the hero of the story, is someone who looks like them? It's not enough to simply have diverse characters in the background; it's critical that your child doesn't just see himself or herself as the sidekick in the story, but as someone who has a strong, powerful, and positive narrative. And the great news is, this applies to all ethnicities, and we live in a day and age with readily available booklists that focus on specific ethnicities—Asian Hispanic Indian, Middle Eastern, and so on. And with the help of the internet, you can get a list of children's books and even request your local library to get access to them. There are many free or affordable ways to gain access to books that honor your child's specific ethnicity.

Are the toys in your home representative of your children's culture? Do the kids have dolls, figurines, games, and so on that honor their ethnicity?

Are the toys in your home representative of your children's culture? Do the kids have dolls, figurines, games, and so on that honor their ethnicity? I cannot stress to you how important it is to surround your children with toys that celebrate their ethnicity, their history, their leaders, and their beauty. (If your BIPOC child is drawn to white dolls or figurines, this is something to dial into because it is more than likely a sign that they have absorbed the message that White is better or preferred. The same can be said for White children adopted into BIPOC homes. If they are predominantly drawn to dolls and toys that don't match their ethnicity, you might want to intentionally encourage and celebrate your child's ethnicity through the toys that you purchase.)

This is common not just in transracial adoptive families, but I've had many non-White friends share about how they face this in their monocultural families too. If you haven't read about the landmark "Doll Test" of the 1940s and the subsequent ones in years afterwards, let me encourage you to spend some time researching and reading about it.[7] But this ideology is enforced if your child is surrounded by toys and other artifacts that don't celebrate their beauty.

Making your home one that is truly inclusive of your children's heritage takes a lot of intentionality, but it's also a lot of fun.

And by the way, this is an issue that monocultural non-adoptive families can address head-on as well. Many children absorb this message because their toys and books all center their family's culture and ethnicity. They believe that their culture, their culture's beauty standards, and their way of life in general is better. If you're a parent or grandparent or just a supporting friend or family member, this is an easy change you can make to help shepherd the children in your life, not just the transracially adopted ones. However, if you are close to a transracially adoptive family or just have a diverse friend group, this will serve any children who are welcomed into your home, whether it be through babysitting, playdates, or sharing a meal together.

Making your home one that is truly inclusive of your children's heritage takes a lot of intentionality, but it's also a lot of fun. It doesn't happen overnight, but ensuring that your child's ethnic culture is represented in the artifacts of your home can go a long way in laying the foundation for a healthy racial identity. It can't be all you do, but it's a great first step.

Tier 2: Representation in voices

When we lived in North Carolina, we attended a multicultural church. But when we moved to West Texas, we had a difficult time finding a truly multicultural church with a diverse staff and leadership. At the time of this writing, we know of some churches with more diverse congregations than others, but a truly multicultural church doesn't yet exist in our area. We have been praying and working toward that end, and in the meantime we've chosen a church family where all our children are represented, but there is still a need for more diverse leadership. As a result, we knew when we moved that we would need to seek out more diverse voices to lead our family.

When COVID-19 hit the United States and shut everything down, we took the opportunity to listen to an additional church online. It was a predominantly Black church that we attend whenever we visit Dallas.

So on Sundays, we'd climb on the couch and livestream a church a few hours away. The coronavirus took many things away, but consistently attending a church that we typically only got to attend a handful of times a year was a gift. It was a truly beautiful season in our family spiritually. Staying at home was difficult at times, but we learned so much during those months. As we sat under the teaching and leadership of that church, some of our blind spots and comfort areas were exposed. We saw how another church handled a global pandemic, protests, and racial division. We saw how faithful exegesis of the text allows for such issues as racism to be discussed in the church.

Here's the thing. Not every cross-cultural adoptive family lives in a city with access to a multicultural church or a church that matches the ethnicity of your child. When we lived in North Carolina, I knew of Korean churches, Hispanic churches, a Chinese church, African American churches, and multicultural churches all within the same general theological beliefs that our family held. But that isn't an option in our current location. So maybe, like us, you choose the best church you can, but you make a conscious choice to listen to other pastors and Christian leaders in addition to your local pastor who can help disciple and lead your family.

The voices you listen to are shaping the culture of your home. I used church as an example, but there are so many other people to help you lead your family—the pastors you sit under, the television that you watch, the podcasts you listen to, or the doctors/lawyers/ school administrators/city council members that you seek out advice from. Your children, *and you,* need voices that are shaping the culture of your home to represent *all* the people in your home.

> *Not only do your children need to see doctors, lawyers, pastors, coaches, and teachers who look like them, but they need to see you placing yourself under their leadership too.*

Our city's mayor and police chief both happen to be Black men, so we pray for them and talk about them. And when they come to visit our children's school or we see them at a community event, we celebrate that and talk as a family how we're so grateful for their strong leadership. Because not only do your children need to see doctors, lawyers, pastors, coaches, and teachers who look like them, but they need to see you placing yourself under their leadership too. They need to hear you listening to podcasts where voices like theirs are teaching you. They need to see you watching or listening to sermons from pastors who look like them. They need their homes, their families, to be places where voices— voices that mirror theirs—are welcomed, respected, and honored.

Tier 3: Representation in community

When we moved to Texas from North Carolina we knew that we would have to be intentional about the community we curated.

It was a significant transition coming from an area where diversity was ever-present, to having to intentionally seek it out in a seemingly segregated area. During our first house-hunting visit here, I knew we were in for quite the transition.

As we drove around town, talking about different areas, our realtor kept pushing us to the southern part of town citing "better schools" and newer homes. After learning about the demographics of the area and the schools, I quickly learned that at that time, the "better" school district in the southern part of town was approximately 70 percent White, 19 percent Hispanic, 4 percent Black, and the other 7 percent composed of small percentages of Asian, Native American, and other ethnicities.[8] When I looked at the demographics of their college readiness programs, not one African American student was enrolled in an Advanced Placement course. In comparison, the city school district was 44 percent Hispanic, 37 percent White, 13 percent African American, 4 percent Biracial, and 2 percent Asian/Pacific Islander.[9] Over two-thirds of the students were considered economically disadvantaged. Ten of the fourteen elementary schools in the district were Title 1 schools (including the one our kids go to). And their Advanced Placement courses had students from every demographic listed.

When I looked into their actual academic programs, I didn't see one that was "better." As someone studying education, what I saw was that one district had fewer people of color and fewer families with low incomes. And the other district was more diverse. One district was majority White and in an affluent area. One district was diverse in ethnicity and socioeconomic status. When we knew we'd be living here for the long haul, we intentionally bought a house that was districted to the city schools.

Now, to be clear, our town isn't a bustling metropolis just bursting at the seams with diversity. It's a midsized town with a small-town feel that living in West Texas brings. We found a home on a small lake, just a five-minute drive from downtown. And we made sure our house was in a community where all of our kids would attend school with people who look like them. We joined city sports leagues instead of predominantly White private teams, and we made genuine friendships along the way. Our community is a vibrantly diverse one as our babysitters, the friends at our dinner table, and the people we do life with reflect a wide variety of ethnicities.

Truly multicultural communities take a lot of work, honesty, grace, and love. But it has been such a joy.

The question we get asked the most by other adoptive parents is, "How do we build genuine relationships with people of our children's ethnicity?"[10] It can be done, and our lives are a testimony to it. If we can do it, two White folks (one from Kentucky the other from eastern North Carolina), anyone can.

It's really simple, and yet, it proves to be the most difficult one for White transracial adoptive parents because it requires you to change what you're currently doing. It's simple because it only requires you to do life in diverse settings. That's really it. The answer is to be present in your community and to be intentional about where you're living your life. It's hard because relationships are always messy, and truly multicultural communities take a lot of work, honesty, grace, and love. But it has been such a joy. Truly, I'm beyond grateful for our friends who feel the freedom to show up for us, but also allow us to show up for them. When I look at the people God has brought into our lives, I feel like I'm the luckiest person on the planet. So when folks talk about how hard it is, I often forget about how initially reorienting your life away from monocultural spaces can be difficult at first.

Sure, it's difficult to swim upstream. It's awkward at first. The changes are hard, especially if you leave a community you've invested in for years. I don't want to undermine the hardship of switching churches, schools, and even friend groups. We've been there. We left a church we adored and joined another church because I couldn't take my children into the kids' program and leave them in a room where they were the only child who wasn't White. And yet, if you're called to transracial or transcultural adoption, you're called to do life in a multicultural community. If you become a cross-cultural family, you cannot live a monocultural life.

HOW IT WILL LOOK

What exactly does this calling look like? I'm glad you asked. We are called to be knowledgeable about schools and churches and sports teams and neighborhoods in our communities. We are called to be intentional about who we invite into our homes and who we spend time with. We can choose where we spend our free time and which cultural events we attend and what relationships we build. We get to choose where we spend our money and, perhaps our greatest resource, our time. And for sake of the welfare and racial identity development of your child, this tier is not optional.

Your child needs racial mirrors not only in the books and toys and voices they listen to, they need racial mirrors that they can touch, see, and talk to. They need to be able to watch and learn from people who look like them and who will have shared lived experiences of being a minority in the United States. And if you're a BIPOC family adopting a White child, they too need people who look like them who they can know on a real and personal level. Children need to be able to cheer on people who look like them and develop real, genuine relationships with adults and other children of their same ethnicity! The adult transracial adoptees who are leading the way in discussing racial identity have made it very clear that books and toys can only go so far, but nothing compares to the physical presence of people.

And not only that, I would add that they need to see families that look like theirs. Some of our dearest friends are transracial adoptive families. In fact, the people we vacation with, the folks we travel to visit and see, and the friends we hang out with regularly all have families that look like ours. It is helpful to not only have deep and meaningful relationships with monocultural families of our children's ethnicity in our direct community, but it's incredibly helpful for our children to not be the only transracial adoptees at our dinner tables. I love that when one of our kids has a birthday party, there are all different types of ethnicities represented, but there are also adoptees (both transracial and same-race adoptees). Even now, our transracially adopted children have a special bond with our friends' transracially adopted children. There is an understanding and a deep love for one another, as they are going through something unique, but together.

The tier that ensures your children have real relationships with people who look like them is the one that matters most.

All three tiers of representation are important, but the one that ensures your children have real relationships with people who look like them is the one that matters most. It's the one that truly helps connect your child to his or her ethnic heritage. The first two tiers are great starts, but the last tier is the one that helps your child create an authentic and sturdy bridge to building a healthy ethnic identity.

Remember, you cannot gift your child a heritage that is not your own, but you can help them build a bridge. And just because you do these three things, it doesn't guarantee that your child won't wrestle with racial identity development. Growing up with parents and potentially siblings who don't look like them will have an impact. The question is, what will you do to ensure that they have the resources and tools and community to help walk beside them through these difficulties?

As parents we want what's best for our kids, and sometimes that means we take a long look in the mirror and reflect on areas where we need growth. Change and growth are hard, but I have no doubt that if you've finished this chapter and are still with me, you can do this.

QUESTIONS FOR REFLECTION

1. Which tier do you feel like you have already incorporated in your life? (If the answer is none, this is a great time to pause and reflect to see if cross-cultural adoption is for you.)

2. What steps can you take this week to grow toward being competent in all three tiers?

3. Take a few minutes to research cultural events in your area. Are there any—within driving distance—that you can plan on taking your family to this year?

4. Where do you need to spend your time, money, and relational capital? What are some things you'll have to say no to in order to say yes to growing in this area?

CHAPTER 7

More Than Love

I am going through a phase where some of my favorite shirts are graphic tees. One is made of a super soft blue material with white lettering on the front: "Love Makes a Family." I enjoy wearing it out in public because we often get questions about our family's makeup, and it's a great way to educate briefly without much interaction.

"Are *all* those kids yours?"

"Why yes! Yes, they are." And I point to my shirt, smile, and walk away.

Love makes a family.

And yet, although "love makes a family" is true, it's an incomplete truth when coupled with the idea that love is all you need. True, deep, lasting love is the foundation of any healthy family. But love that sustains a family has more nuances than a blind, surface level assumption that it's all we need. Love isn't some suffocating euphoric emotion where only rainbows and sunshine and unicorns live. Rather than hunkering down and claiming it's the only thing necessary, love does the opposite. It comes in and makes room for more emotions, actions, and space for people to flourish and grow.

Love is what fuels our pursuit of being a true multicultural family with different colored skin tones represented in it. Love is what motivates our decision to seek out trauma-informed counselors. It's what makes space for our children to walk through complex emotions like grief and loss, rather than insisting they be thankful for being a part of our family. Love is what fuels us to truly love and honor our children's birth families. Love is a commitment that through it all, we are going to stick it out together and weather the storm.

Love makes a family, but it makes room for so much more than just belonging to each other. It makes room for each of us to flourish. It makes room for other virtues to thrive. This world sells us a lot of misconceptions about what love should look like, but Scripture says,

> If I speak in the tongues of men or of angels, but do not have love, I am only a resounding gong or a clanging cymbal. If I have the gift of prophecy and can fathom all mysteries and all knowledge, and if I have a faith that can move mountains, but do not have love, I am nothing. If I give all I possess to the poor and give over my body to hardship that I may boast, but do not have love, I gain nothing. *Love is patient, love is kind. It does not envy, it does not boast, it is not proud. It does not dishonor others, it is not self-seeking, it is not easily angered, it keeps no record of wrongs. Love does not delight in evil but rejoices with the truth. It always protects, always trusts, always hopes, always perseveres. Love never fails.* (1 Cor. 13:1–8)

Love is patient. It's kind. It doesn't boast. It's not self-serving. It looks out for the interests of others. It's not resentful.

These are the characteristics I as a parent want to emulate for my children. I am far from perfect and don't want to give off the idea that we're just nailing this parenting gig in our house. We're far from it. But Scripture guides us even with our imperfections.

So let's flesh this out practically. When one of our kids asks to call their biological mother, love isn't jealous. When one of our children starts to wrestle with difficult questions about being Black in a White family, love is patient. Love is kind. It rejoices in truth-telling. When one of our children wrestles with being Biracial and developing their racial identity in a world that might see them in a different light, we wrestle too. Love bears all things, believes all things, hopes all things, endures all things.

Adoption isn't opening up your home, letting a child in, and hoping that your parental love is enough. It's loving a child so much that you're willing to go meet them where they are.

This sounds beautiful, but true love? It's hard work. It's gritty. It carries the load. It believes in you when you don't believe in yourself. It hopes goodness and mercy for you when you can't hope for it yourself. It acknowledges the loss and holds space for grief and joy to commingle. It endures the hard days and celebrates the good.

And when you apply these theological truths to a cross-cultural adoptive family—that's a powerful picture of God's love here on earth. Adoption isn't opening up your home, letting a child in, and hoping that your parental love is enough. It's loving a child so much that you're willing to go meet them where they are, and together you and your family wrestle and rest in the love of an almighty God until we meet Jesus face to face.

Don't get me wrong. I believe that love makes a family, but love alone can't sustain a cross-cultural adoptive family. You'll need a lot more than just love in your toolbelt, and I don't want to leave you hanging. So here are a few areas where love alone will fail you if you don't allow it to fuel you to get help.

ATTACHMENT

When I first became a mother, I was given all sorts of parenting advice. All of a sudden everyone's experiences in parenthood were deemed the gold standard, and yet I noticed that often the well-meaning advice from a trusted friend would be in direct contradiction of another trusted friend's counsel. Here are a few examples:

Let your baby cry it out, it's good for them.
Never let your baby cry for longer than seven minutes or it will mess with their brain chemistry.
Be sure to have tummy time, but don't let them sleep on their tummy.
Pacifiers are life-savers. Pacifiers will spoil your child.
Breast is best, except when it's not and then this brand of formula is best.
Start feeding your child baby food as early as your doctor allows you.
Do not give your baby pureed food; only feed them when they can feed themselves.
Be sure to wear your baby all day in order to increase bonding.
Do not wear your baby because those wraps are bad for their spine.

Oh. My. Word. I'm exhausted from just writing all that out. You get the point. Our experiences are varied and our opinions are strong, but our unique journeys don't need to be pitted against each other. Rather we can use our unique stories for support, encouragement, and catalysts for further learning. I say all of that to say this: I pray that these next few paragraphs will be that for you. I don't want them to be some standard that you measure your attachment by; rather, I'm hoping these stories serve as a catalyst for attachment with your child.

Before I became a mom, I was worried that I wouldn't be very motherly. I was never the type who dreamed about becoming a mom and quite honestly, children annoyed me. (Kind of ironic for a mom with lots of kids, isn't it? What can I say, the Lord has a sense of humor.) Throughout my pregnancy I would lie awake, rubbing my belly, reflecting back on my high school science class when I learned that some animals in the wild eat their young under certain circumstances. I was terrified that I would be that type of mom, a bad mom, a selfish mom, one who eats her own to save herself. Late at night I would beg God that I wouldn't be that kind of mom. So I listened to all the advice, read all the books, and hoped and prayed something would stick and I would become a nurturing mom.

And then it happened. Amid the trauma of an emergency C-section, I laid eyes on my babies for the first time and something stirred within me. The birth of my children was very physical, but in addition to the actual birthing, there was a tangible maternal energy that I had never experienced before. Maternal attachment was a biological response to birthing my children.

Not a Given

And yet, I have friends who have had children biologically and they didn't have this response. Their attachment had to grow with time. They've whispered over cups of coffee that something just hadn't clicked. The mounds of advice they received wasn't working and their experience didn't match up with that of others. The reality is, attachment and motherhood can be beautiful experiences, but they can also be tainted because we live in a fallen world.

The same is true with adoption—especially cross-cultural adoption.

Babies don't enter the world with a clean slate. Science shows us that babies can feel pain in the womb. It was once estimated that they could only feel pain during the latter portion of the pregnancy, but a recent study says otherwise. Two researchers, one pro-life and one pro-choice, set out to explore the possibility of fetal pain. Their conclusion? "Overall, the evidence, and a balanced reading of that evidence, points towards an immediate and unreflective pain experience mediated by the developing function of the nervous system from as early as 12 weeks. . . . We no longer view fetal pain (as a core, immediate, sensation) in a gestational window of 12–24 weeks as impossible based on the neuroscience."[1]

In *The Primal Wound*, Nancy Verrier argues that babies feel the pain of the absence of their first mothers. She also argues that babies can identify their mothers at birth, and they also experience the grief and loss when separated from their mothers, even at birth.[2] The implications of this are endless. But when the natural process of attaching to your first mother is broken, attachment to your second (and in some instances third, fourth, and fifth) mother is going to look different. It is critical that you acknowledge that if you've adopted (or are adopting) a child from infancy, toddlerhood, or an older child, attachment and bonding look different than a traditional birth, because your child has experienced tremendous loss. And although love is a great place to start, you'll need more than love in order to bond and attach with your child.

When I first met our sons, I looked into their faces and saw zero physical resemblance to mine. I remember rocking and singing to them, looking deep into their dark eyes wondering what they were thinking and feeling. Even though we were strangers, my love for them was strong. And yet, they had to get used to me. I wasn't the voice they were used to hearing. My heartbeat wasn't the backdrop to their months of life in utero. I was a stranger holding them. If you adopt an older child, that list can continue. First steps, birthdays, and major developmental milestones are missed. The loss extends beyond the months in utero and days after delivery.

When we brought our sons home, we felt very attached to them, but that attachment needed to be nurtured in order to grow into true bonding. They had to learn that not only was I the person who fed them, but I loved them deeply. I was safe and I wasn't going away. They needed more physical touch and holding so they could learn our smells, the beats of our hearts, and the warmth of our skin. We minimized guests during those early months and didn't allow non-family members to feed them.[3] The rites and rituals of welcoming an adopted child—whether it's a transracial adoption, same-race adoption, or transcultural adoption—are just different.

The fierce love of a parent is what fuels a commitment to attachment during adoption. You'll need more than love to foster attachment, but it's love that gets you there.

I've met women who said they walked into an orphanage and had an immediate connection to their child. I've met others who have whispered in shame that it wasn't immediate. We have now welcomed four children in our home, and each of their attachments was unique. And yet, my love for them is equally fierce.

There is no shame; you are not less of a parent because your attachment takes work and it takes a lot more than just love. It's not an indication that your love is lacking. Rather the opposite can be said. The fierce love of a parent is what fuels a commitment to attachment during adoption. You'll need more than love to foster attachment, but it's love that gets you there.

You see, pride says you should be able to do this on your own, but love says that you'll lay down your pride and ask for help. Love says you're committed to grow and change and provide exactly what your unique child needs.

There are many different approaches to fostering attachment and depending on the type of adoption you'll use a different set of tools, but my biggest piece of advice would be to invest in an adoption-informed counselor and resources and start there.[4] But whatever you do, I need you to know that attachment in a cross-cultural adoption requires more than just love.

TRAUMA

One of the beautiful aspects of being an adoptive family is getting to know others who have walked similar roads. The adoption community can be an amazingly supportive group of friends and family you can turn to.

When we lived in North Carolina, we were members of a large church with a supportive Orphan Care and Prevention Ministry. One afternoon, I was grabbing coffee with a friend who had adopted internationally and she opened up about the hardships they faced their first year.[5] Through tears she reflected back on their struggles as she wrestled with the highs and lows of the previous year.

Their child had night terrors, meltdowns around food, and uncontrollable tantrums. Attempts to control the child only seemed to escalate the situation. They tried everything, but their child was suffering. Even after a good day, the child would wake up thrashing, terrified, and crying uncontrollably in the middle of the night. The mother, exhausted from months of interrupted sleep, said to me, "I was so tired. I'm still so very tired. But I just keep thinking about how it must be so scary for him to wake up and see White faces, in a strange place, with strange smells, a different language and cultural norms, when he's used to living in a completely different country surrounded by people who look like him."

Because she had done her research before adopting cross-culturally, she knew that when a child experiences loss and trauma, high levels of stress hormones such as cortisol can produce symptoms that mirror Post Traumatic Stress Disorder.[6] She knew that her child had experienced great trauma and loss before setting foot on American soil, and she knew that her child was currently experiencing the trauma from a loss of culture and the loss of being surrounded by people who were racial mirrors.

So rather than suffering in silence, my friend sought out trauma-informed counseling. She read books on trauma, sought out the right professionals (counselors, therapists, social workers), and she and their family changed their lives so their new family member could grieve and eventually take steps toward healing.

In *The Body Keeps the Score*, Dr. Bessel van der Kolk states, "traumatized people become stuck, stopped in their growth because they can't integrate new experiences into their lives."[7] This is why I am a firm advocate for trauma-informed counseling for adoptees and adoptive families. It is traumatic to remove a child from living in a community with a surplus of racial mirrors, and then place them into a community where they are the minority. This trauma, in addition to the trauma they faced from losing their first families, let alone any trauma they experienced while living in either institutionalized care or foster care, can have serious long-term implications on their physical, emotional, and spiritual well-being. Children who lived through extreme hunger, abuse, abandonment, and who witnessed violence— even as young children— have physically experienced trauma. And trauma, as Dr. van der Kolk notes, impacts the entire human body.[8]

Adoption, being separated from your first family and placed in another family, is traumatic in and of itself. But the trauma that a child faces prior to being placed in their forever family can vary depending on circumstances. Here is a non-exhaustive list of traumatic experiences that are common in adoption stories:[9]

Death of a parent/s
Being placed in an orphanage or institution
Abandonment
Verbal, sexual, physical, and/or emotional abuse
Witnessing domestic violence

Neglect

Being placed in and removed from multiple families

Negative foster care experiences

Prenatal drug and alcohol exposure

Poor nutrition pre- and post-birth

Prematurity

Failure to thrive

Lack of proper healthcare

Lack of proper physical needs met (housing, food, having toys stolen or lost during moves, and so on)

If you're adopting a child of any age, even an infant, it is imperative that you become familiar with trauma and its impact on a child. Licensed counselor and author of *The Science of Parenting Adopted Children* Arleta James says this, "Any adoptee—infant, toddler, preschooler, school age, tween or teen—can present with the residual effects of trauma, including attachment problems, because complex trauma starts early in life—in the prenatal period and shortly after birth. The myth of adopting a baby or a young child to have a 'healthy' child must be shed."[10]

> *When a child is in crisis, when they are wounded and hurting, loving them without helping them process their pain seems awfully silly. And yet, for many years the message of "love is all you need" plagued the adoption community.*

This might be difficult, especially if the road that led you to adoption was infertility. However, it's important that we don't allow the roads that lead us to adoption blind us from the realities that we might face. If you're a prospective adoptive parent and this paragraph is hard for you to grapple with, let me encourage you to process this with a licensed professional so you don't unintentionally bring your trauma and grief from infertility into the adoption process.

Trauma doesn't always manifest itself in the exact same way. Not all cross-cultural adoptees experience the same symptoms as my friend's child. But it's important that you understand early on that love isn't a quick fix for trauma. Love can produce an endurance and perseverance to ensure that your child will get the tools and help they need to process their trauma. In *When Helping Hurts: How to Alleviate Poverty without Hurting the Poor . . . and Yourself*, Steve Corbett and Brian Fikkert say this in regard to poverty work (but I think it could be applied to trauma as well): "If we treat only the symptoms or if we misdiagnose the underlying problem, we will not improve their situation, and we might actually make their lives worse."[11] Love can serve as a catalyst for you to change the way you parent, change your routines, and to reach out for help. Love can help you see that these children are so much more than victims of trauma. But "just love" won't be enough to get you through trauma. In fact, it might actually make it worse.

It reminds me a bit of the theological concept that faith without works is dead.[12] We can have all the faith we want, but if we don't live out that faith and act on it—what good is it? What purpose does it serve? After all, our works are proof of our faith. And so is the same for actions and love. Our actions are proof of our love, and not just any kind of love. No, for the adoptive parent, our love is informed, it's intentional, it pushes us to take action.

For example, when a child is in crisis, when they are wounded and hurting, loving them without helping them process their pain seems awfully silly. And yet, for many years the message of "love is all you need" plagued the adoption community. That message has slowly lost some of its popularity, but it still exists in many pockets within the adoption community today (and it definitely exists with those who are unfamiliar with adoption). And so, if you are involved in adoption in any way, shape, or form, it is imperative that you outright reject that mentality. Love is a many-splendored thing, but when it comes to adoption, it takes more than love.

This one chapter cannot fully explore the many complexities of trauma and attachment in adoption. But in this note are some recommended resources for you.[13]

ACTION

When our girls first started school, I'd get them ready and Ben would drop them off on his way to work. Then I'd get the little ones ready to take to preschool. At some point during the chaos of the morning I would try to carve out a few minutes to pray over them. Now, before I give you the wrong idea, you need to know that at the time of writing this book, we have four kids. Getting any number of them out of the house with all the papers signed, lunches made, and shoes on the right feet (most of the time) feels like a miracle. So if you're imagining a put-together mom, praying over her very calm and quiet children while they sweetly eat the breakfast she prepared for them, go ahead and toss that idea out.

Our mornings include a frantic mom running around getting things ready while the kids eat their cereal and milk that they generously poured into the bowl (and all over the table). At some point, the above-mentioned frantic mom, who's still in her pajamas, tosses backpacks to the kids saying, "All right, kiddos, you know the deal! I love you to the moon and back. May God bless you and keep you today. May He give you eyes to see and ears to hear. May He give you hands and feet to go and do His will. May He grant you a love for the things He loves, and may He keep you from sin. Love you big, kiddos! Have a great day! Oh shoot, come back, your shirt is on inside-out!" This was our house most mornings during their early years of school. The point is, this prayer that I pray for my children is also what I pray for adoptive families.

Becoming a healthy cross-cultural adoptive family requires one to move beyond good intentions and focus on good impact. In order to do this, you'll need eyes to see and ears to hear. Our faith requires us to go and do (remember, faith without works is dead). And true love, a love that is pure and reflects the love of God, requires us to love the things He loves and hate the things He hates. I pray these things over my kids, but I pray also for adoptive families because unless we have eyes to see and ears to hear, we are going to miss opportunities to truly love and meet the needs of our unique families. We're going to miss out on loving our closest neighbors—the family God has given us—and our children will suffer because of it.

Dear reader, I'm praying that God gives you eyes to truly see the needs of your child, ears to listen to them and other adoptees and adoption experts, and hands and feet to go and seek out the help and resources your family requires.

So, dear reader, I need you to know that as I type these words I am praying over you now. I'm praying that when it comes to adoption, the Lord gives you a supernatural amount of wisdom. I'm praying that God gives you eyes to truly see the needs of your child, ears to listen to them and other adoptees and adoption experts, and hands and feet to go and seek out the help and resources your family requires. I'm praying that your heart would learn to love the things God loves and that it would be quick to repent of any sin. I hope your home will be a place of shalom, where joy and grief and confession and repentance are all welcome.

And yes, I'm praying for love, but remember, cross-cultural adoption requires so much more than love.

QUESTIONS FOR REFLECTION

1. When you first started learning about adoption, did you think that love would be all that you needed? If so, where do you think you learned that from and what do you need to do to unlearn that idea?

2. If you're an adoptive parent, look at the list of potential traumatic experiences listed in this chapter. Which traumas have impacted your child/children? Are there additional traumas that they've faced?

3. Based on your answer to question #2, what is one action step you can take this week to find a resource for your family to address your family's specific needs?

4. If you're a prospective adoptive parent, what action steps can you take this week to prepare for the journey ahead?

ADOPTEE VOICE

by Daren, Biracial Transracial Adoptee

What Makes All the Difference

Have you ever lost a sock? Or better yet, do you have a single sock in your dresser that doesn't quite match another? Maybe it's a sock that you really like, so you don't throw it out: one with a swoosh or with a unique pattern. Maybe it's one of those 1980s tube socks with three colored bands at the top that have come back in style. Maybe you wear it with other socks that are similar, hoping that no one will notice when it's covered up by pant legs. Perhaps you are holding on to it because you *know* that its match is *around here somewhere* . . .

But that lone sock that just doesn't quite *match* continues to stand alone.

It's ironic that exhausting a metaphor would seem particularly pertinent to this task of writing about one's childhood. This should prove difficult for anyone. The highs and lows of adolescence are daunting, and when you add a "transracial adoption" in there, the pressure seems to build. How do you speak on behalf of a minority group, explaining your experience to the majority?

I am the older of twin boys: thirteen minutes the senior. Our biological mother was Caucasian and our biological father was Black. After being abandoned by our (single) mother, we lived with our maternal great-grandmother until we were eight. After her untimely death, we were shuttled off to our (Caucasian) neighbors for about six months while the state tried to figure out what to do with us. We were eventually adopted by our White maternal great-uncle who lived several states away. (I would be remiss to skip over the fact that our first eight years with our White great-grandmother were fraught with an unhealthy level of physical abuse.)

Our uncle was a lifelong bachelor and an accomplished engineer in his mid-forties. Having left his parents' home at eighteen, he'd spent the majority of his life on his own, and was a bit of an introvert. After hearing the voice of God, specifically through the story of Moses, he felt called to adopt these Black great-nephews of his who lived four states away, even though he never thought he'd be a parent, much less a parent to eight-year-old Biracial twin boys. But we were lost and he was searching. He was someone who had been searching his entire life.

The prospect of twin Biracial sons moving in with this single White man, who had only met each other on two prior occasions (we visited for Christmas twice), and you'll get a unique experience. Throw in a tight-knit faith community (his church home) and his sixty-hour workweek as an engineer, and you'll have our strange family gumbo. Our family was loved and supported, but it was always a little different. My experience as a half-Black kid enrolling in a 95 percent White private school (at the time) where I would attend from third to twelfth grade was more than a little different.

Writing about racism is a tough topic for me. Now as an almost forty-year-old man, I've felt as if my Biracial complexion lives somewhere between a blessing and a curse. I don't remember the first time I felt blatant racism but I certainly remember some jarring experiences.

There was walking into the all-White church, tardy. It was deep in the South, and as two little Black boys entered with their White great-grandmother, we were asked to leave shortly after we'd made our way toward a pew near the front of the church.

There was a girl in English class who raised her hand and talked of the "sin of mixed children," surely unaware that I was four chairs behind her and that I was "mixed."

There was the time a father of the girl I was dating asked that I break up with his daughter. "You know, we really like you, but eventually there could be grandchildren and that just wouldn't be right."

Many Biracial kids who grow up in a mostly Caucasian culture live a discombobulating existence. More often than not I am either seen as "too White" or "not Black enough." Sometimes trying to explain what it is like growing up in the midst of the complexity of this identity seems impossible.

Biracial adoptees often feel as if both resolution and reconciliation are their burden to bear. That is, to make everyone feel more *comfortable* in issues of race, all the while having strong feelings of guilt should they question or feel confused about their identity. Many times, I have found myself the butt of my own jokes regarding racial issues, hoping to make those around me feel less awkward about our differences.

Much has been written, researched, or said about the parental side of this relationship, *but think of the confusion of the child.* Though clearly different, they *naturally* want to be like those who are providing for them, loving them, and raising them. They realize they look different and the nature of that difference lies in complexion. While they are loved and valued, they often feel as if they do not quite *fit.* That they aren't a *natural* part of the family. That they stick out like that single sock that has lost its mate, its family.

Of course, they know they should feel grateful for their family, but there are moments when they look around, and all they see are complete "pairs." Sometimes (maybe even many times) they are made to feel special. Other times, they are that extra sock in the drawer, making life a lot less efficient because they don't "match." It's a lot easier to get ready for work when you have a matched pair of socks than when you have a sock that looks different. To carry the metaphor further, no matter what sock you pair it with, *it will continually experience things differently.*

It's an odd thing to measure the feeling of "family" in terms of efficiency but oftentimes transracial adoptees feel as if they are putting more pressure on their family unit. More pressure leads to less efficiency. Less efficiency makes it feel as if something is out of place. *You* are out of place.

For adoptive families, it's important to know that at some point your transracial adoptee will begin to feel a pressure to both act as everyone else in your family while also identifying with the culture that is thrust upon their stereotypic identity from others. This is especially true if they find themselves in the position of being the only "other" in their community. Preparation and mindfulness will be important disciplines as openness and honesty guide you as you raise these special additions to your family. Growing up, there were moments in which I felt as if my presence complicated every situation. That is, though I knew I was loved, I knew also that I was different. For families, this difference, this inefficiency, this mismatch, isn't the danger—rather, it's how this feeling is handled.

For me, it made all of the difference.

CHAPTER 8

Adoption: It's Not about You

Recently my husband and I spoke at an information meeting for hopeful adoptive parents at a Christian adoption agency. We were on a panel that fielded questions on everything from having an open adoption to what it's like being on a waiting list to creating an adoption look-book.

Our family believes that no question should be left unasked, because even if it exposes something ugly, that ugly needs to be addressed. At one point, a question was asked that showed a lack of empathy for the difficulty of the adoption journey for birth parents and adoptees. My spirit was stirred to speak the truth boldly to this group. I knew that many were hurting, and all they were thinking about is how they could bring their child home. Many of them had longed to be parents for so long. Others, in their zeal for adoption, had lost what was most important.

I've been there.

I've spent nights dreaming and praying for our future children, while neglecting to pray for their first families and for God to intercede on behalf of scared, single, expectant mothers. I remember a season when the excitement of adding to our family overshadowed the reality that adoption is birthed from brokenness. And I remember the night it dawned on me, that as I was "praying my baby home," I was actually praying for a hardship so unthinkable for another human: a birth family and our future child. The night that revelation hit me changed my prayers forever. No longer did I pray for our waiting period to be shorter; rather, I prayed for there to one day never be a need for adoption. I prayed for a world where mothers were able to healthily and wholly care for their children. I prayed for the day when Jesus would right every wrong and children would no longer be orphaned, in need of foster care or adoption.

I need you to know that I, too, have so many times gotten it wrong. So, when I was asked a question that centered the adoption experience around the feelings of adoptive parents while neglecting the feelings of first families and adoptees, I didn't look down on those prospective adoptive parents, because I had been in their seats before too. Instead, I counted it an honor to speak truthfully to them about our journey, just as I am sharing with you today.

Regardless of what brought you to consider adoption, adoption is not about finding a child for your family. It's not about fulfilling your longing to parent. Adoption isn't about you at all. It's about finding a family for every child. And when I told that group of prospective adoptive parents that truth, I saw some shake their heads in agreement, and others have a perplexed look on their face.

So I want to say it again: Adoption isn't about you. It's about finding a family for every child.

"NOT LOOKING TO YOUR OWN INTERESTS . . . "

Part of our unhealthy tendencies in the adoption world is to focus the bulk of attention on the adoptive parents. There are many reasons this has happened. Some of them intersect; others are independent of each other. But one of the main issues is that adoption, as a whole, is a business and the paying customers are adoptive parents. Now, I understand that if you're a foster care family, this might not feel like the case, and so much has shifted in the adoption world in the last decade. But still, there is the reality that adoption is financially transactional and, more often than not, the people paying are given more power.

This is not an indictment on adoption agencies who have to work with—and often pay fees to—other countries, as well as to lawyers, social services, hospitals, doctors, and so on. Rather, this is a mere acknowledgment of the power dynamic. And the history of this power dynamic influences today. It is simply a sad reality that the people who are given the most choice in adoption are the adoptive parents.

Now I want you to pause before you say, "But the children are too young to know what's best!" or "Well, technically in foster care they are given a decision." Instead of explaining this situation away, sit with that reality for just a moment. The children—the adoptees—are the ones who usually don't have any or much choice in a decision that has a great impact on their future. Birth parents are making a choice for them and their child, and adoptive parents make the choice to adopt, but adoptees have little or no say in the matter most of the time. Over the last few years I've met and talked with adult adoptees, and this has been a common theme. This lack of control or power over the beginning of their story is something that has haunted many of them.[1]

This should grieve us deeply, and although I don't have a solution, as an adoptive parent I'm comfortable with acknowledging this dynamic and then working to use my power for the good of adoptees and birth parents, not just for myself. And as a prospective adoptive parent reading this book (or an adoption ally), it is important to recognize this dynamic and then work toward ensuring that all members of the triad can share equal power.

Philippians 2:3–4 says, "Do nothing out of selfish ambition or vain conceit. Rather, in humility value others above yourselves, not looking to your own interests but each of you to the interests of the others."

This is a powerful word for adoptive parents. Do nothing—not even caring for orphans and widows—out of selfish ambition or vain conceit. Don't do anything in order to draw attention to yourself or elevate yourself on the backs of others.

PEOPLE, NOT PROJECTS

A lot of times in church culture, people with specific needs become ministry projects. And when people become ministry projects, we end up lifting ourselves up as experts rather than fellow journeyers. We make ourselves saviors instead of fellow saints.

This applies to the adoption world as well. When we make birth parents, orphans, or at-risk children "ministry projects" and make adoptive parents and adoption workers heroes, we center ourselves as saviors.

Adoption isn't charity work. It's about living your life in such a way that honors all in the adoption triad.

I love that when Jesus was teaching us how to pray He told us to not be fame-hungry people who want to stand in front of others praying so we could be seen (see Luke 18:9–14). But instead, we should humbly pray, "Our Father in heaven, hallowed be your name, your kingdom come, your will be done, on earth as it is in heaven."[2]

If you read the Lord's Prayer in its entirety and full context of the four Gospels in the New Testament you'll see that "thy kingdom come"—to use the stately and familiar language of the traditional King James Version—is not about being the hero of the story or taking pride in a multitude of public ministry projects. When Jesus talks about the kingdom in Matthew, we see an upside-down kingdom in which the first are last, where true leaders aren't kings but instead servants. We see that "thy kingdom come" is about seeing people flourish and thrive and experience the same redemption we've received in Christ. It's about bringing the goodness of heaven here and now for all. Marlena Graves says it this way in *The Way Up Is Down*: "A life emptied of our own agenda in favor of God's is a powerful presence, a servant life, never limited by our education, privileges, worldly possessions, or lack thereof."[3]

Adoption isn't charity work with adoptive families playing the role of hero. It is a servant life that requires great humility, listening, learning, repenting, and, for the Christian, reliance on God. It's about living your life in such a way that honors the flourishing of all people involved in the adoption triad because Jesus, in all His goodness, loves the birth parents and adoptees just as much as He loves me and you.

God, forgive us of our sins as adoptive parents, and deliver us from the great temptation to make adoption about us.

TAKING THE FOCUS OFF OURSELVES

We humans have the tricky habit of making ourselves the center of the story. From the beginning of time when Satan sold Eve the lie that God was keeping her from being like God, we've been unable to keep our eyes fixed on the truth that this life is not about us. We are not the center of every story.

In adoption, there are many ways you can use your unique position in the adoption triad to ensure that every member in the triad is receiving the same honor, dignity, respect, and power that many adoptive parents naturally receive. This list isn't exhaustive, but my hope is that it serves as a catalyst for you to find yourself in a triad where equality, dignity, respect, and power are all shared beautifully.

Listen to adult adoptees

One of the first things you can do when you're starting the adoption process is to start learning from adult adoptees. There are many transracial adoptee podcasts, books, and social media platforms. Many adoptees are currently speaking out and seeking reform. Listen to them. Learn from them. If you have genuine questions, send them an email and ask them if you can pay them a consultation fee for their time and work. But don't put pressure on them to speak on behalf of all adoptees and every adoption situation. Allow their stories to speak for themselves without getting defensive as an adoptive parent.

The point is, there are a plethora of ways you can learn from adoptees, and if you're involved in transracial adoption and you want to have a more balanced view of adoption as a whole, you're going to need to listen to other members of the triad even when it makes you uncomfortable. In fact, I'd say that the areas where we are most uncomfortable are areas we need to press in, listen more, and spend some time in prayer and reflection. That is why adoptee voices are highlighted throughout this book. I invite you to sit with their stories with gratitude and humble hearts.

Honor and prioritize birth families

When our family first started the adoption process, I had not given much thought to birth families. I was so laser-focused on the goal of every child having access to a safe and loving home that I neglected to think about the ramifications and heartache that a birth family faces. I failed to look at adoption from all the different angles, and that's on me. However, once you know better, you do better—

right? Mistakes are a part of the journey, but we have to repent and learn from them if we want to do better.

Regardless of whether you foster, foster-to-adopt, adopt domestically, or adopt internationally, your child has a biological family. They have biological parents, grandparents, siblings (potentially), aunts, uncles, and cousins. They might not have *all* of those, but they have people who share their DNA and their cultural heritage.

This is a powerful blessing and isn't something that should be erased. Instead, it's something that adoptive parents need to foster and figure out ways to connect. Listen, this is tricky. I get it. Out of all the questions we get about adoption, we get the most about open adoptions.

But the thing is, even if you have a closed adoption or if you have an international adoption with limited or zero knowledge, you can still honor a child's birth family. Birth families aren't people or stories that we erase. They are people and stories that we honor and cherish.

Again, this can be difficult in some situations (especially for those who have seen the hardship and trauma that your child has experienced in their first families). But still, it can be done. Honor doesn't mean that we sugarcoat the hard parts of our stories. It means that we look at them through eyes who have seen grace and been changed by it. It means that we hold fast to the truth that all people are broken and in need of a great Savior, and that no one is exempt from that. It means that when we talk about birth families, we speak about them truthfully with humility, love, grace, and great care.

Sadly, there are some extreme situations where all ties with immediate biological family need to be severed. Even when this is the case, we don't talk disparagingly about our child's first family.

Sadly, it also needs to be said that there are some extreme situations where all ties with immediate biological family need to be severed. When a child has been abused and their first family is unsafe, honoring your child's biological family looks different than it will in other types of situations. Always make these decisions with guidance from your social worker and trauma-informed counselor. For some people, that might mean staying in contact with a biological aunt, uncle, grandparent, or sibling. For others, all ties to biological family must be cut. Even when this is the case, we never talk disparagingly about our child's first family.

We want to protect and steward the connections that we do have so that when our children are older, they get to choose what they want to do with their unique birth family relationships.

Partner with an ethical adoption agency

Over the years we've had quite a few friends and acquaintances reach out and ask us questions about starting the adoption process. My greatest piece of advice is always this: partner with an ethical adoption agency.

Here's where it gets tricky. When I talk about partnering with an ethical adoption agency, sure, I am saying don't partner with organizations that are explicitly evil. But this piece of advice is less about agencies that are explicitly evil, and more about avoiding agencies that are implicitly biased. What I'm really saying is to do your work to find an agency that values all members of the adoption triad equally. Ensure that the agency that you partner with uses their finances in a way that doesn't prioritize adoptive families, but instead prioritizes the well-being of everyone involved in the adoption process.

For example, "birth parents" do not all fit into an identical description. They come from various backgrounds and have unique stories. But whatever path has brought them to the point of considering adoption needs to be addressed. An adoption agency should be equipped to connect birth mothers and fathers to the resources they need. Agencies should have strong long-term plans for birth mothers post-placement. And they should have plans for supporting single moms who decide to parent. This doesn't mean that they take care of everything in-house within their agency, but they should have staff who are connected to drug rehabilitation centers, pregnancy support services, counseling services, and affordable housing.

This is just one minor example to think through. But here are some of the questions we asked when we were looking for an agency to partner with (this list is not exhaustive and is a combination of many lists we've collected over the years):[4]

Can you give us a line-by-line breakdown of the adoption fees?

What type of support is offered to birth families post-placement?

What type of care is offered to expectant moms while they're considering adoption?

What type of care is offered to moms who choose to parent?

What type of ongoing support and counseling is offered to birth parents, adoptees, and adoptive families post-placement?

Do you offer adoption education classes? If not, what organizations do you recommend for further learning?

Do you offer transracial and/or transcultural adoption training?

How many adoptive families are on your waiting list? How many adoptions did you complete this last year?

How many paid staff members are adoptees or birth parents?

Is there a discrepancy in the cost of adoption depending on the ethnicity of a child? (If there is, let me just go ahead and encourage you to cross this agency off your list.)

How many failed matches have you had in the last five years?[5]

How do you support the single mother once she's decided to parent?

Will the expectant mother have her own caseworker? Or will we
as the adoptive parents share one? If we share our caseworker,
how do you avoid conflicts of interest?

Does your agency work in community development and family
preservation in addition to offering adoption services? (This
is an especially important question for international adoption agencies.)

(Especially for international adoption): Do the children in the
orphanages have any living family members who would be
able to care for the child if poverty weren't an issue? Can this
information be confirmed?

Again, this list isn't exhaustive, but an agency's responses to these
questions will show you what they value. They might not have the
perfect answer to every question above—and that is okay! But the
goal is to see what they value, where they spend their resources, and
what other organizations they are partnering with. Plus, these questions will help you find agencies that do their best to value all members of the adoption triad equally. This not only helps us ensure that
our adoptions will be ethical, but also the agency you choose helps
serve as a guide in the adoption world. You want to make sure your
thoughts and practices are being led by adoption workers who are
going to care for you, your child, and their birth families with the
highest level of ethics and compassion.

KNOW YOUR PLACE

The other day we were talking with a couple who had just started the
adoption process and the wife announced, "Well, I feel like I already
understand a lot about adoption since so many of our friends have
adopted." I smiled to myself, because I once sounded a lot like her. I
read so many articles, blogs, and books, and besides, I was connected

to so many adoptive families that I truly felt I had a good handle on this whole transracial adoption thing.

Joke's on me.

I remember that a year into our adoption a friend asked me, "Okay, so what is it like being a White mom to a Black baby?" and I just started tearing up as I confessed, "I read all the books and attended all the classes. And nothing can prepare you for the utter heartbreak you'll experience when this world isn't as safe for him as it is for you. I just don't know if I'm doing it right or if I'm screwing it all up." This was not the answer she expected, but it was honest and true.

I thought I understood transracial adoption before we adopted. But now that we've adopted, the more that I learn causes me to realize that there is so much more to learn. And I've also learned that I only hold one of the three necessary perspectives in order to get the whole picture in the adoption triad. Without the other two perspectives of the triad present, we get a skewed picture of adoption. We see it from a limited viewpoint. Every participant in their unique adoption triad must realize that they cannot be the know-it-all in their adoption triad. No, we all show up to our unique adoption triads as individual participants with perspectives that need to grow and change.

Every adoption is unique, and so blanket statements and simplistic "three-step articles" might feel good to read (or write), but even this book will miss the mark with some of you. There will be parts that don't fit for your family—and that is okay because all adoptions are unique. And even though I have studied, read, and written on adoption for quite some time now, I am not an expert. I'm simply a participant with a limited viewpoint. We must know our place, and understand how our role impacts others in order to avoid making this about us.

QUESTIONS FOR REFLECTION

1. Read Philippians 2:1–5 again. What are the characteristics of those who have been united in Christ? List them.

2. How can you apply those characteristics to your adoption journey?

3. Do you have the tendency to make things about you or do you have the tendency to make it all about everyone else? What do you need to do in order to make sure your personal tendencies serve your child instead of wounding them?

ADOPTEE VOICE

by June, Chinese Transracial Adoptee

One Could Never Replace the Other

One of my dearest memories is my mom tucking me into bed at night. She would sit on the side of my twin bed and we would talk, usually about that day or about what was planned for the next day. Then she would pray with me and turn the lights out. I remember one of those nights in particular when we talked about my birth mother. My mom reiterated the story of how I came to be adopted, that I was found abandoned at a bus station in China before being taken to an orphanage, then placed in foster care, then adopted by her and my dad. I remember my mom explaining China's one-child policy to me, telling me that my birth mother probably did not have a choice but to leave me and hope someone would find me. That night we prayed for her before I went to sleep.

Now that I am older, I can barely begin to imagine the trauma and turmoil my birth mother went through that day at the bus station in China. Sometimes I do wonder if she stayed and watched me from a distance, or if she left as quickly as she could, or if she had someone else leave me because she could not bring herself to physically do it. I wonder if she thinks about me often or if she has tried her best to forget and move on. I wonder if we look alike. Though, the one thing I wonder the most is if she gave me a name and what it was, as the Chinese name on my adoption records was given to me by the orphanage.

As I was growing up, my parents always spoke positively about my birth mother. They assured me that she loved me and did what she had to do for me. I remember praying for her on several occasions. My mom always promised me that if I ever desired to find my birth mother, she and my dad would do whatever was possible to help me. While that is something I have chosen not to pursue, I am grateful for their support.

I would encourage all adoptive parents to speak well about their child's biological mother/family, if possible, and even support a relationship with the biological family, again if possible and appropriate. There is no need for my parents to feel threatened or fear being "replaced" if I were to find my biological family. One of the unique aspects of adoption is the fact that there are indeed two mothers who are part of the child's life. When adopting a child, you are becoming a part of that unique adoption "triad." One mother gave birth to me, the other raised me—and one could never replace the other.

Part 3

"WHEN YOU KNOW BETTER, DO BETTER"

CHAPTER 9

Adoption Allies

We've all heard it takes a village to raise a child. And that's true.

But it takes a specific village to raise a transracially and/or transculturally adopted child—it takes adoption allies. It takes allies with eyes wide open to the unique joys and sorrows that adoption brings. It takes allies who are willing to lay down preconceived notions on how to parent and discipline and thrive. It takes allies who are willing to do more than donate, people who will come alongside families and ask, "What is helpful? How can we support the flourishing of your family?" Friends and family of adoptive families, this is where you come in.

My guess is that if you're reading this book, you care. Maybe your child or a dear friend gave this to you to read in preparation for the journey they're about to go on. Perhaps you're a pastor or youth pastor or a ministry leader with adoptive families you're shepherding. Perhaps you are the grandparents or aunt or uncle or cousin or friend from church. Whatever brought you to these pages, let me commend you: we're glad you're here. Your mentorship, your presence, your support matters in our families' lives.

And your impact is holy work. Be assured of that.

So let's dive in. This chapter is going to be a bit different than the others: full of pointers, fewer stories, and perhaps a bit more sass. But I hope the transparency and content serve you well.

RECOGNIZE THAT ADOPTION IS DIFFERENT AND ASK HOW TO HELP (AND NOT JUST ONCE)

Having a child biologically and adopting a child are two very separate paths to building a family. The rites and rituals of having a biological child are usually celebratory. [1] When a couple becomes pregnant and they announce their pregnancy, congratulations are in order. Families celebrate; social media posts are shared; sometimes even parties are thrown. Baby showers are planned. Gifts are bought. Plans are set in place for a hopefully healthy and smooth birthing experience.

When a child is placed for adoption, the road to their forever family is a grievous one that is not in sync with their adoptive parents' experience of the process. Whether a child is removed from a parent, a parent chooses to place them in an adoptive family, or a child is orphaned, all of these roads have their share of trauma, loss, and grief. We don't celebrate this brokenness in the same way we do a typical pregnancy. Growing a family through adoption instead of a typical pregnancy is just, well, different. So, the rites and rituals have to be different as well, even if the adoptive parents' excitement in meeting their child is the same.

When we adopted our fourth child, our church family was incredibly intentional in how they could serve our family. They knew that what they did for typical growing families would be different, but they didn't want us to feel slighted since we were growing our family through adoption. As a result, they offered to celebrate in many of the same ways they celebrated other church families. They asked if they could bring meals, which many adoptive families love, but this didn't really seem to be something that would serve our family since we were going to be focusing on attachment and privacy (and since my husband works in the restaurant industry, dinner isn't typically a need for us). Instead of insisting, they respected our wishes and asked us how they could better support us.

Once we were matched with an expectant mom, the women wanted to celebrate our growing family and so they offered to throw a baby shower, which was an incredibly kind gesture. And I have to admit, I have been to a lot of church celebrations in my life (perks of growing up a preacher's kid), but I especially love wedding and baby showers! It's not because of the delicious food and gifts, but because of a sweet tradition where one of the hosts prints off dozens of Scripture cards specific to that person, and we all take one to pray over them. I get emotional every time we lay hands on a dear sister's belly and proclaim God's truth boldly over her and the life she carries. When they asked, as much as I wanted to say yes, I knew this wouldn't be a good option for our family and so it grieved me to say no.

Bringing a child into a family via adoption is different from bringing a child into this world biologically. And since we were doing a domestic infant transracial adoption, we chose to not have a shower for a baby that wasn't yet ours. We wanted to make sure the expectant mom at the time, who is now our son's birth mom, had the space and freedom to make the best decision for her and her son.[2] And we knew that she could and should be able to change her mind at any point leading up to the day she terminated her own parental rights. We didn't want to add any pressure or guilt by having a

Instead of getting gifts for us, they brought gifts for our adoption agency's housing for expectant moms and birth mothers. Their willingness to celebrate in a way that honors all parties of the adoption triad meant the world to me.

shower. Instead, after I explained our convictions, the women offered to throw a shower for us after we were placed with our son.

So when our son was a few months old, my mom came to town and our friends gathered at a friend's house. A group of women had decorated with a theme that was special to both me and our son's birth mom. The intentionality behind every detail moved me to tears. We ate delicious food and my sweet friends took turns praying over our son. They used Scripture to guide their prayers for him, for his birth mom, and for our family. And instead of getting gifts for us, they brought gifts for our adoption agency's housing for expectant moms and birth mothers. Their willingness to celebrate in a way that honors all parties of the adoption triad meant the world to me. It is a memory I will treasure forever.

And this is just one example of many. Our church family has gladly walked beside us in our adoption, even though it was new to them. Our friends and pastors have graciously told us, "I don't know what exactly to do here, but we'd love to support you in whatever ways you need" and then they listened and showed up. Was it weird to do a shower after a child was born and bring gifts for women they'll never meet? Maybe. But they did it anyway.

You see, although every child should be celebrated, the rites and rituals that we use can be—and in many way should be—different when it comes to adoption. And since every adoption is unique and has its own story, there isn't a clear list of what to do and what not to do. Rather, the best advice for adoption allies is to ask.

And on that note, don't ask just once. The adoption process typically gets a lot of the attention, but the truth of the matter is, for most adoptions there are many needs after placement. Although adoption is a moment in time when a government declares a couple or individual the legal guardian of a child, the attachment process, building a healthy racial identity, navigating loss and trauma, and figuring out relationships with birth families and/or birth cultures are all lifelong journeys.

Offer your help during the adoption process, and then ask a few months later. And then ask again, and again, and again. "Hey, just checking in. Is there anything we can do as a church/as your friends/as your family to support you right now?" As families navigate issues like racism, trauma, loss, ethnic identity, it is a blessing to have the support of family, friends, and church family. We appreciate being seen, known, and loved—but please remember, we need more than love.

Ask often how you can help, and don't be surprised if what they need looks different from the rites and rituals of a typical family.

Not all adoptive families are the same. Some families may need meals and appreciate showers. I have friends who honored the requests of expectant parents and held a shower for the child, knowing that if for some reason the first parents decided to parent instead of placing their child, the gifts they received would go with the child. How beautiful is that? The point is, ask often how you can help, and don't be surprised if what they need looks different from the rites and rituals of a typical family.

POINTERS FOR USING
HEALTHY ADOPTIVE LANGUAGE

I remember when we first started the adoption process how important learning proper adoptive language was. I felt like every time I spoke I would use the wrong term or say the wrong thing. And I remember the constant educating of our family and friends once we brought our first son home from the hospital. The number of times I was asked about his "real mom" was disconcerting. "I'm his mom; I think you were referring to his birth mother, and yes, we both are very much real moms who each play unique but equally vital roles in his life." Honestly, it was exhausting. Although I expected it from strangers, it was hardest when insensitive questions and comments came from people we love.

Consider this:

> The tongue is a small part of the body, but it makes great boasts. Consider what a great forest is set on fire by a small spark. The tongue also is a fire, a world of evil among the parts of the body. It corrupts the whole body, sets the whole course of one's life on fire, and is itself set on fire by hell. (James 3:5–6)

What a powerful visual for how your words can bring death. Just a small spark can cause a great fire that causes doubt and insecurity in a child's life. Too often when we are met with a request to change our language, we respond with pride or defensiveness.

But it's a gift when a brother or sister in Christ invites us to use language that honors them. It's an invitation to speak life and use words that bless, edify, and encourage, instead of using words that have the potential to cause harm. For example, "Gracious words are a honeycomb, sweet to the soul and healing to the bones" (Prov. 16:24), and "The tongue of the wise brings healing" (Prov. 12:18b).

With these words in mind, one of the easiest ways you can love and serve the adoptive family in your life is to learn healthy adoptive language. This concept simply means that you use the correct terminology and use phrases that talk about adoption in an accurate and helpful manner. This might sound like such a small thing, but truly, it can have a tremendous impact. Using proper language honors the dignity and worth of all people involved in the adoption process. It protects the humanity of adoptees, birth parents, and adoptive parents alike. Here are a few pointers to help get you started.

Pointer 1: *The trauma from an adoptee's past is sensitive information and you are not entitled to it.*

It is natural to be curious about a person's origin story, but please know that if you are close to the adoptive family and you ask a question, they may respond with something like, "I'm sorry, we're not sharing those details because we want to honor our child and allow them to be in charge of who gets to know the difficult parts of their story." Don't be offended by this, and don't feel awkward. A great response would be to choose to affirm the parents and say something like, "Oh wow, I didn't really think about that. That makes complete sense! Thank you for being honest with me and helping me look at it from that perspective."

And if you're not close to the adoptive family, please don't ask. Voyeurism is a common practice in the adoption world. And even if an adoptive parent is an open book and hasn't progressed in their journey yet, a child's trauma should never be a feel-good story to ease your curiosity.

Pointer 2: *Do not use "real mom" or "real dad" when talking to adoptees or adoptive parents.*

If you are curious about a child's biological parents and are close enough with the adoptee and/or adoptive family, you can simply refer to them as "birth parent, birth mom, birth father, bio mom, bio dad, first family," and such. Different families will have different practices and honestly, language changes with time, so you can take your cues from them. On that same note, although I am very much my children's real mom, our adopted children's birth parents are also very real.

Pointer 3: *Ethnicity is to be celebrated, but not tokenized.*

I cannot count the number of times acquaintances have said to me during the adoption process, "Oh, are you going to get a cute little Black baby? Black babies are just the cutest!" And I've had friends who have adopted Asian and Hispanic children who have experienced similar questions.

There are many things wrong with this type of statement, though it's likely well-intentioned. For starters, adding a child to your family is not like picking out a pet. The ability to pick out your preferred "type" of child is not something to be celebrated—it's one of the many things wrong with the adoption systems in our country (and I am so grateful to have worked with agencies that have done their best to limit this type of consumerism in adoption). Every time someone says this I try to reply gently: "All babies are beautiful because they reflect the image of God, and we look forward to meeting the child God brings to our family."

All babies are beautiful because they reflect the image of God.

In addition, ethnicity is something to be acknowledged and celebrated, but it's not something that we should commodify. For example, one time I had a teacher say, "I'm so excited your son is here because now our class is more diverse!" You might be trying to express welcome, but it is actually commodifying our children to serve your needs rather than welcoming them and serving them.

As we already discussed, celebrating ethnicity as a transracial adoptive family is something that we should try to do well. And it means the world when our churches, families, and friends get on board with that too. Some helpful ways to do that is to choose to see their differences rather than pretending to be color-blind and to honor their unique ethnic heritage. If you need more ideas, let me encourage you to look back to chapters 3, 4, and 6 and apply many of the same principles to your life as well.

Pointer 4: Never ask "How much did he/she cost?" or say something like "Well he/she sure did cost a lot."

For real, never ask that. Ever. And please for the love of all that is good and holy, do not ask this question in a public place or in front of children. Again, adopting a child is not like buying a pet, a car, or a new computer. Our words matter, and this question objectifies a human.

Our biological twins cost us a lot of money because of two NICU stays, my hospitalized bedrest, and health complications pre- and post-partum. And we have never been asked, "Okay, so how much did they cost?" Please do not ask that question of adopted children.

Now, if you're considering adoption and have questions about the financial cost, do the work and contact an adoption agency or a foster care agency. Many of them have costs on their websites, but they also have informational meetings and staff who can answer those questions and more. If you are close enough with an adoptive family and have genuine questions about finances that cannot be answered via google, a better way to discuss this would be to say, "We have questions about the financial aspect of starting adoption; would you be willing to share your journey with us?"

Pointer 5: Please don't joke about placing your children up for adoption when you're annoyed with them.

Adoption isn't a joke, and it isn't a form of punishment for children. When children who have been adopted hear jokes like this, it's possible for them to internalize this and think that *their behavior* is the reason for their adoption. They can believe that message and start to wonder if it is their fault that they're separated from their biological family. This is especially important for adoptees who have little to no information on the reason for their adoption.

Pointer 6: If you don't know the family,
please resist the urge to comment on their family makeup.

If you see what appears to be a cross-cultural adoptive family at the grocery store, a restaurant, or a school function, that is not the time to come up to them and tell them that you have a "friend/cousin/college roommate/neighbor/grandchild who was fostered/adopted." Honestly, if you feel the need to say anything at all, "You have a beautiful family" is great. But keep in mind—they might not all be family.

On the opposite side of that coin, please do not ask adults if they are babysitting when you see them with a kid with different skin color. They could be their biological parent, they could be an aunt, they could be a foster/adoptive mom, etc. Families don't have to match; however, not every diverse group of adults and children are family.

Pointer 7: "Adopted is a past-tense verb."[3]

One of the unique things about being a transracial adoptive family is that our children's adoptions are obvious. However, it's important to note that our children, after adoption, are simply our children. We have to deal with the long-term issues that come along with adoption. We don't pretend it never happened, but we don't label our children with it either.

We had a unique journey to becoming family, but they are all equally our kids.

With that said, it's helpful if you don't introduce children as "adopted." If you are a grandparent or a family member, this specifically pertains to you. Please don't introduce your grandkids as, "These are our five grandkids, and these two are adopted!" I understand that some families do this out of excitement and celebration, but the specification isn't needed because our kids are just our kids. When you introduce your family you wouldn't say, these are our three blonde children and here is our brunette child.

This analogy isn't perfect, but the point is, their adoption does not have to be the thing that is verbally declared over them with every introduction. Our family has biological children and adopted children. We had a unique journey to becoming family, but they are all equally our kids. We don't need to constantly point out their unique journey, especially one which includes so much loss.

Pointer 8: Representation matters!

If you're a Sunday school teacher or a family member or friend who frequently babysits, try to select curriculum, toys, books, Bibles, TV shows, and movies that include diverse selections.

When we moved from North Carolina to Texas, I was nervous when we put our older son in his first year of preschool. God was so kind to have provided two amazing teachers, and when he came home with a little craft of a child with brown paper skin instead of white, I wept with gratitude. When I thanked them for seeing our son's skin and celebrating it, one of them shared that she had fostered children and her last placement was an African American boy around our son's age. I stood in awe of God giving our family exactly what we needed our first year in Texas. One would think that teachers would be sure to include a variety of skin types, but I can't tell you how many times we've left classes with our Black son carrying home White paper people.

Pointer 9: Impact is greater than intent.

I've alluded to this concept throughout the list of pointers, but I think it's important for you to notice the trend. The impact of your actions and words supersedes your intentions. It is a very common practice for people to dismiss a correction by saying, "Well, I didn't mean it that way!" or "Oh, my intention wasn't to hurt you!"

Those acknowledgments are good and true, and yes, they need to be said. Intentions are not completely null and void, but the impact of our words and actions is more important. If you don't mean to cut someone, but you end up cutting them anyway, they're still bleeding regardless of your good or bad intentions. Our focus shouldn't be on whether you meant to hurt someone, it should be on helping the hurt individual heal. When an adoptee, a birth parent, an expectant mom, or adoptive parent tells you that your church, school, class, words, systems have been harmful to them, your first response shouldn't be "I didn't mean to . . . " It should be, "I'm so sorry. Please, tell me more."[4]

Since we live in a fallen world, even our good intentions can lead to harmful impact.

This concept should be a freeing one that all believers can identify with when confronted with harmful impact to adoptees. Rather than spending our energy defending what we meant or intended, we can freely recognize that we made a mistake because we believe that "all have sinned and fall short of the glory of God" (Rom. 3:23). We can acknowledge that since we live in a fallen world, even our good intentions can lead to harmful impact. We boldly proclaim that Jesus came to save sinners, of whom we are the worst! We don't use our fallen nature as an excuse, but rather we use it as a starting place for reconciliation. Where there is brokenness, heartache, and hurt in this world, we model Christ's redemptive character and work hard to bring life, healing, and restoration. And we cannot do that if we are so focused on our intentions that we miss the damage of our impact.

MORE THAN ADOPTION ALLIES

I don't know if you noticed, but many of these pointers don't require any money or honestly much effort other than learning and choosing to lay down an old way of thinking about things in order to serve someone else. Paul says in 1 Corinthians 8:9, "Be careful, however, that the exercise of your rights does not become a stumbling block to the weak." Stephen Um says it this way in his commentary on 1 Corinthians:

> Christians are able to enjoy freedom because someone sacrificed his freedom on their behalf. Their rights are the result of Christ laying aside his claim to any and all of his rights. Our liberties are ours because the ultimate stronger brother gave up his liberty to secure the liberties for his weaker brothers, namely us. . . . Christ did not die to save the solitary individual; he died for his bride, his collective people, his church. *Rights are never exercised in isolation, because they always have a bearing on those around us. We must never miss the sociological implications of the cross. It's not a question of what one can or cannot do. It's a question of how to serve others and live a life that makes the gospel compelling.*[5]

If you're a Christian friend or family member supporting an adoptive family, you are more than merely an ally—you are brothers and sisters in Christ who are learning how to serve others and live in a way that shows the transformational power of the gospel. When you take the time to learn and to serve the transracial adoptive families, birth parents, adoptees, and foster families in your lives, you are telling a true and better story in a society that values individualism, rights, and personal freedom. When you value the flourishing of others and are willing to change your life for the good of that flourishing, you mirror Christ's love for us spent on the cross. When you lay down your freedoms so that others might live more freely, you are displaying the love of Christ for your sisters and brothers.

This is what takes mere allyship from a basic level to a familial one. In Christ, we weep with those who weep and rejoice with those who rejoice. Our Christian family is one who carries the wounds of others and lifts the arms of the weary among us. Your support of adoptive families isn't just a really good thing to do; it's what Christ would do and has done for us.

And so, dear brother or sister in Christ, I'm so glad you're here. I really am. And if you made it to the end of this chapter, I want to thank you for doing the hard work of examining what you can change to better support the transracially adoptive family in your life. Change is hard work, but it's the work of all who are a part of the family of God.

QUESTIONS FOR REFLECTION

1. If you're an adoptive parent, who in your community needs to read this chapter? There are many people who are eager to come alongside your family in your adoption journey. Perhaps one way of inviting them in would be to gift them with a copy of this book and ask them to specifically read this chapter.

2. If you're a family or friend of an adoptive family, what is one new thing you learned from this chapter that you can start applying right away?

3. What is one rite or ritual that you might need to change or abandon altogether in order to support the adoptive family in your life?

4. As a follower of Christ, what is something you can do to help ensure that families who are adopting are supported?

CHAPTER 10

Responding Well: The Power of Words

A few years ago, right after we had first adopted, we were visiting San Antonio's beautiful Riverwalk and had stopped to eat at a delicious Tex-Mex restaurant right on the water. We sat outside, with our three kids (at the time) and watched the boat tours pass by. Our daughters were four and our son was about six months old, and our family stood out.

Now, anyone who has had identical twins knows the experience of standing out all too well. Everywhere we went with our blonde, blue-eyed, identical girls, someone was commenting. But you add transracial adoption to the mix, and when our crew was little, well, it was a lot.

Our girls giggled with fresh excitement every time a new boat drove by and they would wave at the tourists. With our eyes fixed on the water, we hadn't noticed that a passerby who was walking along the boardwalk had made their way to our table. Out of nowhere, a

IT TAKES MORE THAN LOVE

woman was standing by our table and said, "Excuse me, but you have
a beautiful family. And may God bless you. What you're doing is a
wonderful thing. You're doing a really good thing." She wanted to
talk more, and we engaged her for a brief moment and then focused
our attention back to the boats to signal that she should move on.

Now, here's the thing. We were new adoptive parents, and I was
just getting my sea legs underneath me. I don't remember how I answered her, but I'm sure I could have responded better. What I do
remember is the sinking feeling that sat in my stomach when she
walked away. I knew that we had to figure out how to respond to well-
intentioned comments like that, and we had to do so quickly before
our son grew up thinking he was some kind of burden and our girls
got the idea that we were some kind of superhero saviors.

Both positive and negative comments are a part of being a transracial adoptive family. Our families stick out and it isn't uncommon
for people to strike up appropriate and inappropriate conversations
while we're out and about.

When it came to people asking questions, I had to figure out which ones genuinely cared, which ones were merely curious, and which ones were voyeuristic and/or insensitive.

Unfortunately, I have dozens of
stories. Should I tell you about the
time at a pizza place a woman made
the racially charged comment that
the only way we were going to fix this
country was to raise "those people's"
kids for them as she patted my arm
and walked away? Or what about the
woman in the grocery store sobbing
to me about some adoption horror
story while my two-year-old listened in? Anyone who has adopted
cross-culturally knows the discomfort of having strangers make
absurd comments, judgments, and questions about your family.

This was so very hard for me when we first adopted, but I quickly
learned that I had to be prepared. Otherwise, I would either find

myself smiling to protect the feelings of strangers, or I would find myself with tears in my eyes from the anger of someone insulting my child's culture or first family. And heaven help the soul who insulted their birth parents. My fierce loyalty for birth families could unleash a whiplashing of words that I would regret once I got to my car. I wanted to respond reasonably and graciously, but also firmly when someone crossed a line. I just couldn't seem to figure it out and always ended up disappointed with myself.

One of the first things I had to figure out when it came to people's questions was which people genuinely cared, which ones were merely curious, and which ones were voyeuristic and/or insensitive. Yes, the type of question was important, but also who was asking it was equally important. People I knew and had relationships with were in a different category than strangers in the grocery store, so although they might have the same question, I would approach it differently.

THREE TYPES OF RESPONSES

One of the courses we took during the adoption process was on being a conspicuous family.[1] The presentation needed updating, but nonetheless, one of the main concepts was that you need to have a lot of tools in how you respond to comments about your family. The training suggested three ways of responding: an informational response, a humorous response, and a response that guards privacy.[2] And I found that each of these types of responses could be used depending on the circumstance and the type of relationship I had with the person.

Informational responses, according to Adoption Learning Partners, are responses that you would use with family, friends, and closer acquaintances that you see. These types of responses are educational in nature, but they still guard and protect your child and family. For example, a relative might ask if you ever talk to your child's real parents. And informational response could be, "Oh yes, we have an open adoption and I talk with my child's biological family, but honestly I want to honor my child's privacy and want them to be in control of who knows what, so we don't like to overshare on the details of that relationship."

As you can see, the response is informative in that it gives just enough information to answer the question, and it is educational in that it gently corrects the family member's language (real parents vs. biological parents) and sets a clear boundary. You cannot expect family and friends to understand every aspect of adoption and many of them are genuinely curious (not voyeuristic like many strangers are). Being informative while setting clear boundaries is a skill that is developed with practice, so it's good to think ahead of some questions that your family and friends might ask and write out strategic responses.

Humorous responses are phrases and replies that are intended to deescalate uncomfortable scenarios.[3] In my opinion, humor only works if (a) your child and their first family are never the punchline, and (b) it fits you and your child's style. Humor can be an excellent tool to comfortably engage and educate strangers and then pivot away from them. But there is a fine line that can quickly be crossed. Adoption isn't a punchline and it's not a joke. So this needs to be approached with great care, but sometimes it's just what the situation needs.

One time we were at a store when the twins and our older son were tiny and a woman came up and said, "Well, well, well! One of these things is not like the others!" and my four-year-olds said simultaneously, "Of course not, we're twins and he's a boy!" Their response quieted my anger, and so I just laughed and walked away instead of reprimanding or educating the woman. The truth is, there are times when education is absolutely needed, but depending on your child or children, it might not be the best every time. Sometimes a little humor and then walking away is exactly what's needed.

Privacy-guarding responses, according to Adoption Learning Partners, are quick responses that are "designed to protect your child and your family, quickly cutting off further discussion."[4] Truth be told, this fits my style and personality well when it comes to dealing with nosy questions from strangers or defending our children's first families. You will need a few privacy-guarding responses already written up and practiced so that when you're in line at the grocery store, you won't stand there flabbergasted or go off in a fit of anger while your kids watch as a stranger awaits your reply.

PREPARED WITH PRACTICAL ANSWERS

As I mentioned, I quickly learned that I needed to have prepared responses in order to protect the dignity of our children and their first families. Over the years, I've jotted down a few that we use regularly. Here are some responses that I have used over the years. Feel free to take and adapt to your liking:

When asked about the cost of adoption from a stranger: "Finances are always a personal matter. We're keeping those details to ourselves." When it's asked about finances by a friend who is considering adoption, "The costs of adoption vary based on the agency and type of adoption you pursue. My best piece of advice is to research the type of adoption you want to pursue and then you can investigate the cost of the organizations that will help you."

When asked about the makeup of our family: "Yes, all these children are ours. Families don't always match, and how each of our children joined our family is a private matter."

When asked where our children are from: "Oh, our family is from Texas." If they push further, "Are you asking that question because some of our kids are Black and Brown? Because Black and Brown people are born in the United States too."

When someone compliments or praises us on adopting: "Actually, we aren't heroes here. We're just the lucky parents of these amazing kiddos."

When someone talks poorly about our children's birth families (yes, I know, this is hard to imagine strangers doing. But it has happened to me multiple times): "Actually, we love and respect our children's birth families, so please don't speak of them that way in front of our family."

When someone asks for information about their birth families: "We so appreciate your concern and care for our children's stories, but that's information that we're protecting so that our kids have the opportunity to choose what type of personal information gets shared and with whom."

When a stranger tells you, "I just can't imagine giving up my child," you can say, "Actually, in my opinion, birth mothers who choose to place their children in safe and loving families are some of the bravest people I've met."

> **Depending on the ethnicity of your child and the stereotypes that exist in your community, you'll need to be prepared to pick out a few sentences to educate and combat these stereotypes in your family.**

If you're sleep deprived and looking to escalate a situation instead of defusing (not that I'm saying that I did that one time . . . but I'm not saying that I didn't say this either), "Well, I can't imagine saying such an offensive thing to a stranger. It looks like we both need to grow in empathy for others." But for those of you who are less bossy and more well rested and don't have open adoptions: "Not all birth parents place their children for adoption. But whatever brings a person to that point, the last thing they need is shame heaped on them."

When someone applies racial stereotypes to your child, it is critical for you to combat that racism. For example, the amount of time our Black son was told that he was going to be an amazing athlete by strangers was absurd. Now, he was a very big baby and we live in Texas, so a lot of people would comment on his "football thighs." But whenever a stranger would say, "Oh, I bet you'll be a football player one day!" or something to that effect, I would always counter it with, "Or a pianist. Or a chemist. Or a doctor. Or a preacher! But just because he's Black and a solid baby doesn't mean he'll play football." Interestingly enough, our second son was also a big baby with some chunky lil' baby thighs (but he's Hispanic and Native American, not Black), and we never had strangers comment on his athletic abilities. Depending on the ethnicity of your child and the stereotypes that exist in your community, you'll need to be prepared to pick out a few sentences to educate and combat these stereotypes in your family.

And last but not least, if I'm shocked by some random comment or question, "I'm sorry, what? I don't think I heard you correctly. I thought you asked about _____, but surely that can't be the case because that's an incredibly personal question to ask a stranger."

Almost all of these are said with a smile on my face and a sweet disposition because I'm southern, but the firmness of my words and posture are clear almost every time. And in most cases, I don't wait around for further conversation. My goal is to end the conversation as quickly as possible and leave. Sometimes that means I say the phrase and immediately walk away to protect my children from a defensive response. Other times I'm more gentle. But when you're an adoptive family, you quickly learn how to discern voyeuristic questions from genuine ones, and although your response might be the same, your posture toward the person might differ.

YOUR CHILD AS THE AUDIENCE

In the book *In On It: What Adoptive Parents Would Like You to Know about Adoption*, Elisabeth O'Toole writes, "No matter who asks the question, or how uncomfortable the circumstances, when you're called upon to discuss a child and his adoption, it's important to think of the child as your real audience. . . . Whenever someone asks me questions about my children or adoption, I try to ask myself, 'What's the best answer—*for my child?*'"[5]

One of the other points that Conspicuous Families training made was that your response needs to honor the personality of your child. Your personality might bend itself toward responding in a humorous way, but if it embarrasses your child or if it makes them feel uncomfortable, that's the wrong type of response. The goal of choosing how to respond is both to protect your child and to teach them how to handle the questions they will receive. It's balancing truth and grace and wisdom and boundaries all while doing hard normal life things like going to the grocery store with your kids in tow.

> *Being firm, setting healthy boundaries, and telling the truth isn't rude. It's a kindness to your child, and honestly, it's a kindness to the stranger.*

Again, you can probably take the sass level up or down a notch according to your personality and the comfortability of your children. But the point is, your family stands out and it will receive comments of all sorts. You, the parent, need to be prepared for how you are going to protect the dignity and worth of your child, their first family, and their cultural heritage. All three methods of responding—informational, humorous, privacy-guarding—are valid and needed depending on the situation, and you aren't going to get it right every time. However, preparation is key to not oversharing and to honoring your children.

For those of you who have a more difficult time being firm with strangers, I want to take a moment to encourage you. I believe what my mama taught me when I was young is absolutely true: being rude is unacceptable and two wrongs never make a right. However, being firm, setting healthy boundaries, and telling the truth isn't rude. It's a kindness to your child, and honestly, it's a kindness to the stranger. Nine out of ten times, I say these statements in a gracious way (again, catch me sleep deprived and some sass might slip out), but you aren't responsible to guard the feelings of strangers when you're merely telling the truth. However, you are responsible to guard the feelings and identity development of your child.

Your words serve as a shield for your children from the many darts that others shoot out of their mouth. Protect them at all cost.

QUESTIONS FOR REFLECTION

1. Of the three types of responses that Adoption Learning Partners recommends, what type do you think will come the most naturally for you? Why?

2. Write a response to the following scenario: You're at Thanksgiving dinner and your cousin comments about your announcement to adopt: "I just love adoption. I really do. I think it's great, but the whole nature versus nurture thing is concerning to me. Do you think your adopted kids will bring their real family's baggage into your family?"

3. When asked questions about your family out in public, who should you be the most concerned about hearing your answer? Why?

ADOPTEE VOICE

by Whitney, Romanian Transcultural Adoptee

Entrusting the Mysteries to the Lord

My story begins on the other side of the world, in the Eastern European country of Romania. The oppressive dictator had been killed on Christmas Day 1989, about six-and-a-half weeks after the Iron Curtain had finally fallen. Just a little over a year later, a nineteen-year-old girl gave birth to me. Due to factors outside of her control, she was unable to raise me, so she made the courageous decision to create an adoption plan for me. As the country struggled to regain its identity, the Western world flooded in after years of being shut out. They brought news cameras and documentary crews with them, and filmed the state of the country. Little did the producers of a *20/20* special on Romanian orphans know that their program would be the catalyst for a North Carolinian couple to make the five-thousand-mile trip to Bucharest to adopt me.

I grew up with five siblings, all adopted internationally. Adoption is normal for me, because it's all I've ever known. My local community included other adoptees, some from Romania, and others from different parts of the world. From a young age, I saw other families built by adoption and learned that even if families don't bear one another's blood or skin tone, they are still family.

My parents were very open with our adoptions, and I felt comfortable discussing my story with my siblings. We were all adopted at different ages, and some of us have more memories of our countries, our stories, and our lives before adoption than others. As I matured, I began to process my story with more depth and complexity. I'm now in my thirties, and my husband and I are in our own adoption process, seeking to welcome a few little ones into our family soon.

I look at my own adoption story and see both the brokenness and the beauty. The reality is, there's always loss involved in any adoption story.

While I was adopted at birth, that doesn't change the fact that there's a break in my story. Anytime there's a fracture in the natural family, loss is involved.

I'm aware of the fact that everyone's experience isn't the same as mine, but I'm learning to hold both the beauty and the broken pieces of my story in tandem.

Additionally, there are parts of my story that remain a mystery to me.

"Who is the woman who gave birth to me?"

"Do I look like my father?"

"Where are they now?"

"Do they wonder about me?"

Each adoptee processes those questions differently, and that's okay.

As I've processed these and other questions, I've learned to entrust the mysterious pieces of my story to the Lord. I may never know certain aspects of my history, but those pieces of me aren't unseen or unknown to the Lord.

Being a Christian changes how I view my adoption story. Scripture tells me that I am an adopted child of God. His Word reminds me that I was known in my mother's womb and chosen before the foundation of the world. Nothing that anyone says or does on this side of eternity can change that reality. There will always be pieces of my story that remain a mystery to me, but the truest thing about me will never change and is secure.

I'm not a mom yet. I'm waiting—waiting to know who our children will be, what they will look like, and what their little personalities will be. Even when I am a mother, there will be pieces of my children's stories that are unknown to me. I won't be able to provide all the answers for them. But I can point them to the One whose love will never fail them, who will never forsake them, and the One whose gaze is set upon them.

And so, I daily pray for my children, asking the Lord to be near and to bind up the brokenhearted, just as He has promised.

CHAPTER 11

Kingdom Eyes and a Holy Imagination

When I was a teenager, I was at a basketball game when my parents were sitting across our small gymnasium waving at me. I didn't wave back. When my mom came over and lectured me about ignoring her, I was clueless as to what was going on. After a few more situations like these, she took me to get my eyes checked. Sure enough, I needed contacts or glasses so I could see.

I remember driving home with my mom from the optometrist with contacts in my eyes for the first time, and I kept saying, "Mom, I can see the leaves on the top of the trees!" It was shocking how much I had missed out on seeing, but once I was given the right prescription, I could see things clearly.

Whenever life gets complicated, I often think back to that moment and I wonder what I'm currently unable to see. Typically when chaos and heartache are present, we only get bits and pieces of the story. Maybe we can see the trunk of the tree and make out some blurry green thing up top, but we can't see the leaves. With adoption, it can be easy to diagnose or prescribe a solution for the small parts we see without fully getting the whole picture. But as Christians, we believe in a God who sees and knows all. He is a God who draws near to the brokenhearted. And so, more often than not, when things get confusing, I ask Him to give me eyes to see people the way He sees people. I ask Him for kingdom eyes partnered with a heart bent toward redemption.

IMAGO DEI

In *The Way Up Is Down*, Marlena Graves pushes us to take a good hard look at the people we tend to ignore: "The people we ignore because they don't seem worth our time and attention? Because they aren't famous enough or at all, aren't rising stars or at the top of whatever game we wish to play? They may be a beggar at the gate of an estate, a janitor, maid, taxi driver, immigrant, elder living alone or in a nursing home, prisoner, or a child. These precious ones could very well be kings or queens in the kingdom come."[1]

In the world of adoption, do we treat birth parents like they aren't worth our time and attention? Do we treat them like they aren't worthy of the same redemption we've received? Do we use them to grow our families, only to ignore their humanity after a child is in our home?

Do we treat adoptees like commodities? Do we treat our children like accessories to our family, brought in to "complete" or make our family happy without ever thinking about what they lost?

Here is the truth we must all come to agree on: every member of the adoption triad is made in the image of God. This concept is central to followers of Christ, and it is the foundation for how we view and treat all people. And we must beg God to give us kingdom eyes so we can live out those truths.

So what impact does this have on the way we view and treat or talk about birth parents? Well, this is a hard question to answer because every adoption is different. But here are a few scenarios that I'll share with you and some examples of what this looks like.

Open Adoption: Honoring *imago Dei* in all parties looks like adoptive parents serving as a bridge between the adoptee and their first family. This bridge looks different in all families, but it is preserving a relationship and striving toward health and wellness. This doesn't mean that you throw all boundaries out the window, but rather it creates boundaries that serves first and foremost the child, and then second the birth family, and then last the adoptive parents. It looks like honoring the contract agreement and making adjustments in agreement with the birth family. This might mean increased contact or less contact (depending on the bio family's requests and adoptee's requests). But in all seasons, a mutual love and respect between adoptive family and birth family should be sought after.

So one of the unique aspects of open adoption, which is the case with our family, is that two moms, with two different life stories, perspectives, and expectations, come together to love and support a child. The way she loves our child is different from the way I do, and that's okay. But make no mistake: my kids' *I've gained so much from learning from our children's first families and from being loved by them.*

birth moms love them fiercely. At the same time, there are a multitude of reasons why it is best for our children to be in our care. I will not divulge those details, but they chose to place their children in a safe and loving home for a reason.

At first, we weren't sure how we were going to navigate this relationship, but our typical prayer guided us: "God, give us kingdom eyes and a heart bent toward redemption." The truth is, I arrogantly went into it with that perspective thinking I would be the one doing a lot of giving, but I've gained so much from learning from our children's first families and from being loved by them. I've been so blessed by being accepted by them in spite of my many failings. As I write this book, I'm counting down the days until our first in-person visit with our younger son's birth mother. She's coming to our house for the weekend and we can't wait.

Over time, our relationships with our children's first families have grown and developed into their own beautiful stories. Their families are precious to me. Their wins are my wins and their losses are my losses. And each adoption has been different. Some relationships are healthier than others, and in other seasons they ebb and flow. But the goal isn't to have the exact same relationship or even to have a relationship that I deem healthy and mutually beneficial. The goal is to love our children's birth families exactly where they are, because God loves them. It sounds a lot prettier in writing, but the truth is, this is holy, gritty work but it's absolutely worth it.

Closed Adoption: This looks like honoring your child's birth family by never speaking ill of them and sharing what information you have with your child. If no information is given, it means taking great care those first days of their lives and gathering whatever information you can and keeping it in a safe place for your child. It means researching and learning about your child's ethnicity and medical predisposition through DNA tests. And then it looks like serving as a bridge to their history (e.g., research, cultural awareness, joining clubs or groups). Both honesty and grace should be your guide when it comes to talking about their first families, and *never* do you help create a narrative that is untrue.

Where there are gaps in your child's story, it is normal for both you and for them to attempt to fill the gaps with a created narrative. Please do what you can to talk honestly about their birth family, but do not cross a line by creating a false narrative (that can be overly positive or overly negative) if you don't have the facts. You honor your children and their first family by pursuing honesty with grace, and by offering your presence with your child when they grieve the holes and missing pieces of their stories. And as your children get older, you support them as they choose whether or not they would like to research and potentially pursue reunification with their biological family.

International Adoption: International adoption is complex, but even where there is little to no information, you can honor a child's birth family and heritage. The way you speak about their orphanage, the workers who cared for them, the city and culture they came from all matters. Their life didn't start when you brought them home. There were days, months, and maybe even years where others cared for them. So ensuring that your child has knowledge (at minimum) and a connection to those who cared for them during their early time in institutionalized or transitional care is another way to honor their birth culture.

Let honor, truth, and grace be your guide. Do not fill the gaps of your child's story with "what ifs," but instead speak honestly about the things you know and the things you don't. But it is important that you don't speak poorly of their culture and their earliest days, while still speaking truthfully about them.

Foster Care: Honoring *imago Dei* in situations where parents have had children removed from their care can sometimes be difficult, and yet we are still called to do it. When an adult puts a child in an unsafe environment, it can be easy to judge them quickly and with little grace. However, perhaps it's better to ask, "What brought this person to this point in life?" Compassion for your child's first family must always be present, even in worst-case scenarios when all ties to birth families must be broken in order to keep a child safe. We can hold space for multiple emotions at the same time. We can grieve the hurt first families have caused, while still praying for their health and wellness and restoration.

We must always protect our children—that is a non-negotiable. But what a gift to our children to know that their adoptive parents believe that no person is too far from the transformative grace of Jesus Christ. Depending on the severity of the situation, perhaps consistently praying for your child's first family is a good first step. For others, maybe pursuing a relationship with a biological aunt or grandparent is an option to honor *imago Dei* in your child's first family. But regardless, you can have compassion for an individual while still acknowledging that their choices are unhealthy and incredibly harmful to your child's well-being.

> *You might be in a situation where none of these scenarios fit. There isn't a one-size-fits-all, four-step list on how to have kingdom eyes for your children's first families.*

And last, you might be in a situation where none of these scenarios fit. There isn't a one-size-fits-all, four-step list on how to have kingdom eyes for your children's first families. Ultimately, it's our hearts that need changing. And fortunately, we serve a God who is in the business of changing hearts. As Marlena Graves reminded us, it should be our hope that our children's first families are kings and queens in the kingdom to come.

GOD'S GIFT: HOLY IMAGINATION

We've already said it—adoption is complex. And complex issues require creative solutions. I'm not sure that all the crises that lead to adoption can be solved this side of heaven. However, that won't stop me from pursuing, dreaming, and asking, "What needs to change here so everyone can thrive?"

Author Sharon Miller once wrote, "Imagination is not a frivolous, liberal pursuit. It is a godly discipline. Without it we will be tempted to rely solely on what we can see, hear and know with our senses, instead of opening ourselves to the greater reality of God, a reality that the small-visioned status quo is unable to grasp."[2]

I love that. Our imagination and reliance on a creative God could change the landscape of the adoption world. I wholeheartedly believe that we need more adoptive parents with a holy imagination and a longing for "thy kingdom come" here and now on this earth.

We need people who are praying life over their children, but also who are praying life and restoration and healing over their first families.

We need families who are willing to step into the foster-care system and be all-in for family restoration.

We need families who will welcome single moms into their homes and walk beside them as they care for their children.

We need churches who don't shame single women for getting pregnant, but who have holy imaginations for what a beautiful life looks like for them.

We need social workers and adoption experts with holy imaginations for how to close the equity gaps in adoption systems and ensure that birth parents are given opportunities to choose life for themselves—not just their babies.

I recently had the privilege of talking with some of the key leaders who are paving the way with policy change and adoption best practices at Bethany Christian Services. Dr. Kimberly Offutt, the Director of Family Support and Engagement, was sharing about some of the training sessions they do for transracial adoptive parents. And when I asked her about some changes she hoped to see in orphan care and prevention in the future, she immediately mentioned that we need an overhaul in the way we talk about adoption and foster care. She was exhibiting a holy imagination in dreaming up better ways we can talk about adoption, foster care, and first families.

Adoption experts and orphan care and prevention leaders are in the dreaming stages, asking, "What can we do to ensure that every child has a safe and loving home?"

Lifeline Christian Services offers holistic care to expectant parents with free counseling and tangible services that meet the unique needs of single parents and birth parents. The small local adoption agency we used when we lived in North Carolina offers a yearly birth-mother retreat for free for any woman who has placed a child through their agency. Our current adoption agency in Texas has housing for women who need a few months to get on their feet. They know that ongoing contact, counseling, and resources are vital to meet the needs of the women they serve. The truth is, there are many adoption agencies who, much like Bethany Christian Services and Lifeline Children's Services, pursue the highest ethical standards while finding homes for children *and* pursuing family restoration.

I've talked to adoption experts and orphan care and prevention leaders all across the country and almost all of them are in the dreaming stages, asking, "What can we do to ensure that every child has a safe and loving home?" Sometimes adoption is the answer, but there is a great need for some holy imagination in family preservation and crisis prevention. They're dreaming and praying and asking good questions, like How do we equip churches and orphan care organizations to come alongside communities in serving families that are at risk for being separated? How do we minimize the need for adoptions to actually take place? How do we keep families together, and provide better support for single mothers? How do we ensure that Black and

Brown children aren't being removed from homes at higher rates than White children?

And as adoptive parents, specifically transracial or transcultural adoptive parents, these are questions we need to be wrestling with too. How can we better the system that has brought our children to our families? How can we be a part of the solution? What role do we have to play? Are there laws and policies in place that need to be changed to better serve birth moms and adoptees? What attitudes or preconceptions do I bring to the table that need to be changed in order to honor all members of the triad?

I don't have all the answers in this book. But what I do know is that in order to make a dent in any of these major issues, we're going to need kingdom eyes and a holy imagination. We're going to need people who love God and are attuned to the work of the Holy Spirit. We're going to need courage to swim upstream when many are content with the status quo. And we're going to need a heart so changed by the love of Jesus that it's permanently bent toward redemption.

"THY KINGDOM COME" PEOPLE

For a long time, I misunderstood the church's role while we are in between Christ's first and second coming. I knew that we were called to go and make disciples and that we should look forward to the day of Christ's triumphant return. But somehow, I missed that we, the church, are supposed to mirror Christ's kingdom full of love, mercy, grace, and redemption in the messy in-between. That we were called to reflect our eternal kingdom, here and now. That belief in Christ didn't just have an eternal impact, but it impacted our present days.

Skye Jethani said in his daily devotional, With God Daily, "The church is supposed to preview the new world God is creating, not preserve the one which is passing away."[3] I love that imagery, and it reminded me of some words that Jesus said when He was teaching us how to pray.

The Lord's Prayer was one that I was always familiar with and loved dearly, but I was in seminary when I realized that I was missing an important piece of the puzzle. I had a professor in seminary who always said of the church, "We are to be 'Thy kingdom come' people!" Typically, when I prayed for "thy kingdom come" I was praying for Christ's second coming, yet I noticed that when Jesus prayed, He was referring to the here and now. You see, we're to be praying for redemption and restoration and goodness and mercy, here and now—on earth as it

> *There is nothing too far gone, too broken for our God. We're to be praying for redemption and restoration and goodness and mercy, here and now—on earth as it is in heaven.*

is in heaven. Our lives, our families, our work should be of kingdom work, not just in evangelism, but in bringing about the redemptive good news that there is nothing too far gone, too broken for our God. Thy-kingdom-come people are, like Skye Jethani said, a preview of what's to come.

When it comes to adoption, I've thought a lot about what it would look like for God's people to work toward eliminating the orphan crisis, the foster care crisis, and so on. Yes, opening our homes and families is a good response. But I wonder if with some kingdom eyes, holy imagination, and a Thy-kingdom-come attitude we could get at the root of the problem?

I dream of a day when the church might just be the answer, not only in welcoming children into our homes, but in preventing the need for children to be removed from their families in the first place. I am so encouraged by Thy-kingdom-come people and churches who are safe havens for women who find themselves with unexpected pregnancies. I'm blown away by churches that are so intimately in-terwoven in pursuing wholeness and the welfare of their cities that their very presence is tied to the success of the marginalized in their communities. And honestly, I'm encouraged, because although not every church is a Thy-kingdom-come church, I believe that we're witnessing a movement among many that are.

And as for the adoption community, I'm seeing it happen here as well. Although adoption will most likely always exist, I pray that one day the world looks a little more like heaven with fewer children being separated from their family of origin. And in the meantime, I am praying for some holy imagination for God's people to be His hands and feet to both the orphan, the single mom, and families in distress.

Lord, let it be so, on earth as it is in heaven.

QUESTIONS FOR REFLECTION

1. What is one area in cross-cultural adoption that you might not see or think clearly on?

2. Other than adoption, is there an area in orphan prevention or family preservation that ignites excitement in you? If not, pray and ask God to give you eyes to see an issue and begin praying about it.

3. What does it mean for God's people to be a Thy-kingdom-come people?

4. How do you pray in regard to adoption? What changes might you make?

A Final Thought: Love Is Still Our Guide

It's ironic with a book titled *It Takes More Than Love* that I want to leave you talking about love. *Although it takes more than love, love is still our guide.* It is the firm foundation from which we build our families. It is what sustains us when we're tired from the journey. Love covers a multitude of sins. Love protects, it trusts, it hopes. Scripture tells us that God is love, and that Love came down and dwelt among us so that we could experience redemption. And friends, while we've talked frankly about the hard and broken aspects of adoption, I want to be sure to leave you with this: **the hard doesn't negate the beauty in adoption because, when done well, adoption *can* bring good out of brokenness.**

It is no small thing that the first and second greatest commandments have to do with love. When Jesus was asked, point blank, what was the most important of the commandments in all of Scripture, He replied, "'Love the Lord your God with all your heart and with all your soul and with all your mind.' This is the first and greatest commandment. And the second is like it: 'Love your neighbor as yourself.' All the Law and the Prophets hang on these two commandments" (Matt. 22:37–40).

You want a home where a child can thrive? Love God and love others.

Sometimes I think we overcomplicate it. But we've been told by the Son of God that love is the ticket. It's the greatest commandment we have. Love God. Love others. And the rest of the commandments hang on these two.

But what does that mean for the adoptive family?

Well, everything.

Parenting ain't no joke. Children, regardless of how they join our homes, need parents who love God and love others. They need to see parents with their Bibles open and their hearts set on Jesus. They need to know that a relationship with God isn't just going to church on Sunday, but it's an everyday commitment to living out our faith. And to an adoptive family, loving God and others truly is the commandment that we hang everything else on.

You want a home where a child can thrive? Love God and love others.

Do you want to create a home where people of all ethnicities are welcome? It starts with loving God and loving others and recognizing the image of God in every human soul.

Do you want a family where brokenness isn't shamed because we have confidence in a God who is with us in the hard parts of our stories? Fix your eyes on Jesus, the author and perfecter of our faith. And as a result, love God and love others.

Do you want your children to know that they are more than their trauma? Love God and love the broken among us. Proclaim the greatest story mankind has ever known: Love came down so you and I, in our brokenness, can taste the sweetness of wholeness of life in Christ.

Love is what fuels our dedication to the conviction that every child should have a safe and loving home. It's what drives us to ethical adoption practices. Love is what enables us to change our parenting styles, and ask for help from licensed therapists and adoption experts. It's what pushes us to advocate for more equitable adoption policies where all members of the triad are honored. Love is what causes us to answer the phone at 3:00 a.m. when we see that first family's number appear. Because we love God and love others, we are unequivocally anti-racist and do everything in our power to teach our children that their identity is in Christ alone. And that truth doesn't erase their ethnic identity, but instead it celebrates it. Our love of God and others fuels the schools we attend, the communities we live in, and the church families we're a part of.

Love changes everything.

Friends, this world will constantly tempt you to put love of money, love of comfort, love of self above everything else. And the adoption world is no exception. We are really good at taking good things and twisting them to serve ourselves. But adoption, and specifically transracial adoption, is something that needs to desperately be rooted in your love for God and love for others.

Hebrews 10:23–25 says, "Let us hold unswervingly to the hope we profess, *for he who promised is faithful. And let us consider how we may spur one another on toward love and good deeds,* not giving up meeting together, as some are in the habit of doing, but encouraging one another—and all the more as you see the Day approaching."

I hope these pages have served you well. But more than anything, I pray they spurred you on toward love and good deeds. I pray that you walk away with a greater love of God, a greater love for others, and that the love you've read about will free you to know that when it comes to adoption, it takes more than love.

Research Tips and Explanation of Terms

And just a few quick things: As I was writing this book, I kept a list of other things that I wanted to try to squeeze in. If you're new to the adoption world, these might not make sense, but they will one day. Just tuck them away for now and research them when the time is right.

PACA (Post-Adoption Contact Agreement). If you have an agreement with your child's birth family or your adoption agency, honor that agreement and send updates as you said you would. Go above and beyond to keep your door to communication open. Even if your child's first family doesn't do their part, always do yours. And if the relationship is strained, for whatever reason, please still do your part and send updates to the agency so that one day, if a first family or birth mom is in a healthier place, they can go there and see you're still there, holding space for them and keeping your word.

Store and document every piece of information you can get about your child's biological, medical, and cultural background. Not everyone gets that opportunity, but when I was in the hospital with our kids I kept running notes with things mentioned, little things and big things. I knew I was too tired and sleep deprived to remember the information later. And it might not all be documented in the paperwork. The same can be said on the visit to the orphanage or transitional care facility if you adopt internationally. Take meticulous notes and make sure you store that information for your children one day.

Names. This is a WHOLE thing. You should research keeping your child's name and why you should or shouldn't. If you have an international adoption, do your best to keep, honor, or incorporate your children's names. If you have an open adoption, consider keeping the name the birth mother gives. In both of our instances, our children's first parents didn't name them and wanted us to name them. The first time we just named our son and the second time we had a list of names and worked through them with our son's birth mom. But whatever you decide, naming is important and often holds significance for adoptees later in life (especially if their name is changed), so be sure to learn from adoptees and first families before making such a big decision.

Here are a number of topics related to racism and racial identity that you should do more research on: cultural appropriation, colorism, racism in hair standards, and imposter syndrome. All these issues are things you should be aware of in raising a child from a different ethnicity.

Laws and policies you should research and know about: ICWA (if you, like us, adopt a child with a Native American heritage), MEPA (Multiethnic Placement Act), FFPSA (Family First Prevention Services Act), ASFA (Adoption and Safe Families Act), ICPC (Interstate Compact on Placement of Children), Adoptee Citizenship Act, Hague Convention, The Intercountry Adoption Act of 2000, the UAA (The Universal Accreditation Act of 2012).

The History of Adoption and Transracial Adoption. If you haven't studied the history of transracial adoption in your country, you should consider spending some time navigating the complexities of your country's adoption (same-race, transracial, and transcultural) laws and how they came to exist. For example, the history of transracial adoption in the United States is fascinating, and in my opinion, there is so much from our past that informs our policies and systems today.

EXPLANATION OF TERMS

The following isn't an exhaustive adoption language list. But it's enough to get you going and should be helpful when reading this book if you're new to the adoption world. There are many language lists online that can be of assistance for you, but hopefully this is a great start!

Adoptee: The child or person who was adopted.

Adoption: "The complete transfer of parental rights and obligations from one parent or set of parents to another. A legal adoption requires a court action." (https://www.adoptivefamilies.com/how-to-adopt/adoption-terms-glossary/)

Adoption Triad (or just Triad): The Adoption Triad refers to the three units of people involved in adoption: Birth parents, Adoptee, and Adoptive parents. It is often depicted in the form of a triangle, where each corner of the shape represents one of the participants in adoption. Often you'll hear people involved in adoption refer to their "corner of the triad" or another corner of the triad. That simply means they are specifically talking to a particular group in the adoption triad. For example, this book is written with a specific corner of the triad in mind: adoptive parents.

Adoptive family: The family unit that legally adopts an adoptee.

BIPOC: A BIPOC person is a person or persons who are Black, Indigenous, and/or a People of Color. Language changes with time, especially language that describes race and ethnicity. However, this term (at the time of writing this book) is used when describing people of color and you are describing multiple races and/or ethnicities, or when you're talking about a population and it isn't possible to discuss their specific race or ethnicity. For example, when I can not specifically name a person's ethnicity, I use that instead. But when I'm talking about a broad range of ethnicities represented by transracial and transcultural adoptees, I use BIPOC if I'm talking about non-White transracial adoptees. However, I don't call them "non-White" as that is centering their identity around Whiteness.

Birth Mom or Birth Mother: A woman who has made an adoption plan and carried it through. This name is reserved for women who have already placed their children for adoption and their parental rights have been terminated; *it is not used for women who are considering an adoption plan.* Adoptive families and adoptees might refer to this woman as mom, birth mom, bio mom, biological mom, first mom, belly mama, etc. Each family is unique and language changes with time, and so when referring to a birth mother, it is best to follow the cues of the family and/or adoptee. One example of this is that when our children were really young, we used the term "belly mama" so our children could understand that they grew in another woman's belly (it was very confusing to one of our sons so we chose this language intentionally). But as they grew in their understanding, we stopped using that language and now refer to her as their bio mom or birth mom. That might change as the relationship grows and our children will later decide what they want to call her and we, the parents, will follow their lead on that.

Closed Adoption: An adoption that is closed in its nature doesn't involve any contact between the birth family and the adoptive family and adoptee. More often than not, adoption records are sealed and any contact between the birth family and adoptive family isn't permitted. However, if any contact is initiated, it must be mediated via the adoption agency or a case worker.

Domestic Adoption: A domestic adoption is an adoption that takes place within the country that you live in, for example, when an American couple adopts a child from the USA.

First Family: This refers to the adoptee's birth family. Sometimes, when children are adopted at older ages and have memories of their birth family, they prefer to identify them as their first family or bio family. Again, our perspective as adoptive parents is to follow the lead of adoptees and birth parents, and to foster a healthy relationship between the two.

Foster Parents: "State- or county-licensed adults who provide a temporary home for children in state custody whose birth parents are unable to care for them." (http://www.families4children.com/adoption_definitions.cfm)

International Adoption: An adoption where the adoptive parents and the adoptee are not from the same country.

Open Adoption: An open adoption is open in its nature, meaning that in some form or fashion there is an open relationship between the birth family and adoptive family. There are a wide variety of open adoptions ranging from sending letters, gifts, texts directly to each other, to also sharing in-person meetings, birthdays, etc. For example, we have open adoptions with two of our children's birth families and they look very different. Our approach has been to follow the lead of our children's birth families and our children in what they are ready for and then to respect the boundaries they need while also doing our best to keep those lines of communication open.

Semi-Open Adoption: This adoption is a lot like it sounds, semi-open. Information is shared between adoptive families and birth families, but it is done through a mediator like a social worker or an adoption agency. Personal contact information is not shared.

Transracial Adoption: An adoption where the adoptive parents and the adoptee don't share the same race.

Transcultural Adoption: An adoption where the adoptive parents and the adoptee don't share the same ethnic culture. It is also referred to as transnational adoption or international adoption.

Transracial Adoptee: Sometimes referred to as TRA. A transracial adoptee is a person who was adopted by a family that does not share their race.

Transcultural Adoptee or International Adoptee: A transcultural adoptee is a person who was adopted by a family with a different ethnic origin. For example, if a White Australian couple adopts a White child from Romania, that child is a transcultural adoptee. However, if a Black American couple adopts a White child from Romania, this is both a transracial and transcultural adoption.

Acknowledgments

First and foremost, thank You Jesus, the author and perfecter of my faith. Thank You for Your promise of redemption and to one day make all things new. May that day come quickly, Lord.

To Ben, Felicity, Noel, Jude, and Zeke—I adore you. Each of you are my greatest earthly treasures and I love you. Thank you for supporting me, loving me, and being the best family a girl could ask for. Mom and Dad, thank you as well for the time you've spent watching our kids and loving on our family so I could write this book. And thank you for always believing in me. To our kids' first families, thank you for choosing us. You are so precious to me and I pray you always know it.

To the adoptees who took time to share their stories and write the essays in this book. Out of all the words written in this book, I pray yours are elevated and taken the most seriously. Your contributions are so near and dear to my heart. I'm so grateful. So very grateful for you. Cheering each of you on in your individual journeys. May God bless you and keep you, may His face shine brightly on you. And may He give you peace.

To the team at Moody who helped shape and launch this book. Y'all are rock stars and I'm so grateful for every person who took time to provide feedback, make edits, design the cover, market the book— ALL OF IT, the work seen and unseen, I'm incredibly grateful for each of you. Specifically, Trillia . . . what would I have done without you? Thank you for asking me to write this book and then for coming alongside me throughout the process. Grateful doesn't even touch how I feel, but since I'm all out of words, thank you will have to do.

To every person who endorsed this book—thank you, thank you, thank you. Thank you for using your influence to help get this book out into the world for the good of our kids and the glory of God. I'm so grateful.

And last, to those a part of the adoption community who are willing to have these hard conversations, who are willing to allow nuance, truth, and grace to be their guide, thank you. Thank you for picking up this book and reading it. I pray that these pages bless your family.

Notes

Chapter 1: Welcome to the Journey

1. This quote by Maya Angelou has been widely used but was popularized by Oprah Winfrey: http://www.oprah.com/oprahs-lifeclass/the-powerful-lesson-maya-angelou-taught-oprah-video at 2:27.

2. Transracial adoptions are adoptions where a child of one skin color is adopted by parents of another skin color (for example, this could be a BIPOC individual or couple adopting a White child, or a White couple adopting a BIPOC child, etc.). Transcultural adoptions are adoptions where a child from one country is adopted by parent/s of another country. BIPOC is the current abbreviation for Black, Indigenous, and People of Color.

Chapter 2: Shedding the Savior Complex

1. A great resource to read for mission trips and a savior mentality is *When Helping Hurts: How to Alleviate Poverty without Hurting the Poor . . . and Yourself* by Steve Corbett and Brian Fikkert (Moody, 2012). Much of what I've learned on this topic has been greatly shaped by this book. Also by these authors is *Helping without Hurting in Short-Term Missions* and other practical resources.

2. Melissa Guida-Richards, *What White Parents Should Know about Transracial Adoption: An Adoptee's Perspective on Its History* (Berkeley, CA: North Atlantic Books, 2021), 19–20.

3. This quote by Maya Angelou has been widely used but was popularized by Oprah Winfrey: http://www.oprah.com/oprahs-lifeclass/the-powerful-lesson-maya-angelou-taught-oprah-video at 2:27.

Chapter 3: Race-Conscious Parenting

1. Beverly Daniel Tatum, *Why Are All the Black Kids Sitting Together in the Cafeteria? And Other Conversations about Race* (New York: Basic Books, 2017), 318.

2. Do not be deceived by the title of Dr. Tatum's book. This book isn't limited to the concepts of race from a Black and White relationship. Chapters 8 and 9 are essential to any transracial adoptive parent as she specifically addresses issues of race and racism from multiple other ethnicities' perspectives. In fact, I highly recommend this book to cross-cultural adoptive families. It's long and somewhat academic, but it's worth the perseverance. And if you're not the reading type, get the book for those specific chapters alone.

3. Tatum, *Why Are All the Black Kids Sitting Together in the Cafeteria? And Other Conversations about Race*, 319–20.

4. This training was provided through Be the Bridge (www.bethebridge.com).

5. Brian M. Howell and Jenell Paris, *Introducing Cultural Anthropology: A Christian Perspective* (Grand Rapids: Baker Academic, 2019), 36.

6. Ibid.

7. Evan P. Apfelbaum, Michael I. Norton, and Samual R. Sommers, "Racial Colorblindness: Emergence, Practice, and Implications," *Current Directions in Psychological Science*, 21(3), June 2012: 205–209, https://doi.org/10.1177/0963721411434980.

8. Retrieved March 16, 2021 from *The Daily Show with Trevor Noah,* https://www.cc.com/topics/cwg3bq/growing-up/l7zl17.

9. Adia Harvey Wingfield, "Color Blindness Is Counterproductive," September 13, 2015, *The Atlantic,* https://www.theatlantic.com/politics/archive/2015/09/color-blindness-is-counterproductive/405037/.

10. Latasha Morrison, *Be the Bridge: Pursuing God's Heart for Racial Reconciliation* (Colorado Springs: WaterBrook, 2019), 23.

11. Trillia J. Newbell, *United: Captured by God's Vision for Diversity* (Chicago: Moody, 2014), 75.

12. https://implicit.harvard.edu/implicit/takeatest.html.

Chapter 4: More Than Haircare

1. Jane Jeong Trenka et al., eds., *Outsiders Within: Writing on Transracial Adoption* (Boston: South End Press, 2006), 27–28. This account is the first part of a four-part essay and was written by Jeni C. Wright. The other portions can be found in *Outsiders Within.*

2. Although I've recommended this earlier in the book, chapters 8 and 9 of Dr. Beverly Tatum's *Why Are All the Black Kids Sitting Together in the Cafeteria?* are a fantastic resource for families who have Asian, Hispanic, Native American, or Indian children.

3. "A Conversation with Transracial Adoptee Bonita Croyle," All God's Children International, podcast February 24, 2021, https://allgodschildren.org/podcast/027-antiracist/.

Chapter 5: Offering Our Presence in the Hard

1. Alison Cook, "The Danger of Bypassing Your Emotions," *Relevant*, September 3, 2019, https://www.relevantmagazine.com/faith/growth/the-danger-of-bypassing-your-emotions/.

2. Ibid.

3. Ibid.

4. For more information, check out Be the Bridge at www.bethebridge.com.

5. When we moved to West Texas, I was certain we'd have to travel the almost three hours to Dallas-Fort Worth to find a good counselor, but lo and behold, when I looked up trained trauma-informed counselors at the Karyn Purvis Institute for Child Development (https://child.tcu.edu/tbri-practitional-list/#sthash.5164Mxsu.dpbs), I realized that a local foster care and adoption agency had counselors onsite for children ages 6+ and they offered play therapy for younger children who qualified. Don't be afraid to travel to find a good therapist—but also you'd be surprised at how many offer virtual sessions, *and* you might even be surprised to find one near you!

6. Margaret A. Keyes, Stephen M. Malone, Anu Sharma, William G. Iacono and Matt McGue, "Risk of Suicide Attempt in Adopted and Nonadopted Offspring," *Pediatrics* 132 (4) (October 2013): 639–46, https://doi.org/10.1542/peds.2012-3251.

   Also, Gail Slap, Elizabeth Goodman, and Bin Huang, "Adoption as a Risk Factor for Attempted Suicide During Adolescence," *Pediatrics* 108 (2) e30 (August 2001): https://doi.org/10.1542/peds.108.2.e30.

7. Jessica M. Hadley, "Transracial Adoptions in America: An Analysis of the Role of Racial Identity Among Black Adoptees and the Benefits of Reconceptualizing Success Within Adoptions," *William & Mary Journal of Race, Gender, and Social Justice*, vol. 26 (3): (2020).

8. *The Adoptee Next Door with Angela Tucker,* season 1 episode 4: Nancee Winslow: "Who Would I Be If I Hadn't Been Adopted?"

9. *The Adoptee Next Door with Angela Tucker,* season 1 episode 8: Kristen Garaffo; "Everyone Just Assumed I Was White." 30 minute 36 second mark.

10. These two resources are great starting points. However, let it be said that although I appreciate the Adoption Networks' age range and many of their suggestions, the birth/newborn age begins centering the adoptive parent in the story. A child's story starts with their family of origin. And that is where we always begin our children's stories. https://adoptionnetwork.com/adoptive-parents/parenting/talking-about-adoption/ and https://www.psychologytoday

.com/us/blog/navigating-the-adoption-journey/201703/how-and-when-discuss-adoption-your-child.

11. Nigel V. Lowe, Margaret Borkowski, Mervyn Murch et al., *Supporting Adoption: Reframing the Approach* (London: British Agencies for Adoption and Fostering, 1999).

12. Again, this is where a trauma- and adoption-informed counselor can help speak into your specific family and your unique adoption story. They will be able to help you develop a plan to foster ongoing conversation in your family.

13. Some people in the adoption community believe that being matched with an expectant mom is malpractice as though it is a form of coercion. I can only speak to our specific adoption, but we were matched early because it was what our son's birth mom requested emphatically. Our adoption agency let us know that this was a rare request and that it came with "risks." She wanted and needed to get to know us extremely well, and so we went into being matched, knowing that until she terminated her parental rights, that sweet baby was 100 percent hers. We chose to use that time to encourage her at every moment we could that if she chose to parent, we would support her 100 percent and that she had the right to change her mind at any moment. And we cherished getting to know her and all our time together, and we believe that time spent together prior to placement has served both her and our son well.

Chapter 6: Representation Matters

1. H.U.E.: *Heal. Unite. Engage. Redeeming the Race Narrative*, episode 1, "Transracial Adoption: How Can I Teach a Heritage That Is Not My Own?" https://podcasts.apple.com/us/podcast/ep-1-transracial-adoption-how-can-i-teach-a/id1310951014?i=1000502666989.

2. Again, I attribute much of what I've learned to sitting under the leadership of other people. Latasha Morrison has an entire organization dedicated to building bridges in racial reconciliation. I love that she uses the imagery of bridge building, and must give her credit here for the concept of "building bridges."

3. Krista Maywalt Aronson, Brenna D. Callahan, and Anne Sibley O'Brien, "Messages Matter: Investigating the Thematic Content of Picture Books Portraying Underrepresented Racial and Cultural Groups," *Sociological Forum* 33, no. 1 (March 2018): 165–85. https://doi.org/10.1111/socf.12404.

4. Rudine Sims Bishop, "Mirrors, Windows, and Sliding Glass Doors," *Perspectives: Choosing and Using Books for the Classroom* (Summer 1990): x.

5. Rudine Sims Bishop, "Walk Tall in the World: African American Literature for Today's Children," *The Journal of Negro Education,* 59(4) (Autumn 1990): 557.

6. Krista Maywalt Aronson et al., "Messages Matter," 165.

7. "Study: White and Black Children Biased toward Lighter Skin," https://www.cnn.com/2010/US/05/13/doll.study/index.html.

8. https://schools.texastribune.org/districts/wylie-isd-taylor/.

9. https://www.abileneisd.org/our-district/district-information/.

10. I want to clarify that this is a question asked by White transracial adoptive parents. This book is for all people who adopt cross-culturally, but in my experience, BIPOC parents who adopt transracially are already professionals at this. They are used to living in diverse settings with a wide variety of people and are used to navigating White culture. It's typically White adoptive parents who often wrestle with this question.

Chapter 7: More Than Love

1. Stuart WG Derbyshire and John C. Bockmann, "Reconsidering Fetal Pain," *Journal of Medical Ethics* 2020, 46:3–6, https://jme.bmj.com/content/46/1/3.

2. Nancy Verrier, *The Primal Wound: Understanding the Adopted Child* (Baltimore: Gateway Press, 1991), 5; also see 18–21.

3. Some in the adoption world call this season cocooning. Depending on the type of adoption and age of the child, it can last up to 6–12 weeks.

4. There are two specific resources I would recommend for further reading on this topic. First, *The Connected Child* by Dr. Karen Purvis. Second, *Created to Connect: A Christian's Guide to The Connected Child*. You can find both of those resources and more at www.empoweredtoconnect.org.

5. Some details about this situation have been changed/withheld to protect privacy.

6. Bessel van der Kolk, *The Body Keeps the Score: Brain, Mind, and Body in the Healing of Trauma* (New York: Penguin Books, 2015), 52–58.

7. Ibid., 53.

8. Ibid., 52–58.

9. Many of these are listed and addressed in Arleta James's book *The Science of Parenting Adopted Children: A Brain-Based, Trauma-Informed Approach to Cultivating Your Child's Social, Emotional and Moral Development* (Baltimore: Jessica Kingsley Publishers, 2019).

10. Arleta James, *The Science of Parenting Adopted Children*, 36.

11. Steve Corbett and Brian Fikkert, *When Helping Hurts: How to Alleviate Poverty Without Hurting the Poor . . . and Yourself* (Chicago: Moody, 2012), 52.

12. James 2:14–26.

13. For further learning on trauma and attachment, I highly recommend *The Body Keeps the Score: Brain, Mind, and Body in the Healing of Trauma* by Bessel van der Kolk. It was a hard read, but an important one. Also, Dr. Karen Purvis, author of *The Connected Child* and *The Connected Parent*, has a center that studies TBRI (Trust Based Relational Intervention). You can read her books, articles, and other resources by visiting www.child.tcu.edu. And again, a Christian guide to

her work *Created to Connect* can be found at www.empoweredtoconnect.org. I also highly recommend *The Science of Parenting Adopted Children: A Brain-Based, Trauma-Informed Approach to Cultivating Your Child's Social, Emotional and Moral Development* by Arleta James.

Chapter 8: Adoption: It's Not about You

1. Again, I want to be careful as to not paint adoptees as some sort of monolithic entity and I do not want to speak on their behalf as a group. There are many adoptees online who have created consulting firms, written books, and share their unique perspectives on social media, and I would like to take this moment to encourage you to seek them out!

2. To read the Lord's Prayer in its entirety, see Matthew 6:9–13.

3. Marlena Graves, *The Way Up Is Down: Becoming Yourself by Forgetting Yourself* (Downers Grove, IL: IVP, 2020), 144.

4. This list isn't one that I came up with on my own. It's a conglomeration of multiple lists that I've read. Over the years, I've reworded them and added some of my own questions.

5. For the record, I don't like the term "failed matches" but it is one that adoption professionals use. Anytime a mother chooses to parent her child, that's not a failure, that's something we celebrate and support.

Chapter 9: Adoption Allies

1. We must also acknowledge that having biological children doesn't always end happily. We live in a world where sin has broken everything. There isn't a thing left untouched by brokenness—including birthing children. To my friends who have gone through difficult pregnancies, to the ones who have left the hospital with empty arms, I see you and I'm sorry. This is not how it was meant to be and I grieve that with you. This example is of a typical, healthy birth and is not meant to pour more salt in your wound.

2. In the adoption world it is respectful to use healthy adoptive language. When a pregnant woman is considering adoption, she is called an expectant mom. Once she places her child for adoption, she is referred to as a birth mom. This gives the woman space to make the best decision possible for herself and her child, without pressuring her to become something she hasn't yet chosen to be.

3. Russell Moore, *Adopted for Life: The Priority of Adoption for Christian Families and Churches* (Wheaton, IL: Crossway, 2009), 189.

4. Along this line, please do not call Black or Brown children "monkeys" or gift them with pajamas or clothing with pictures of monkeys on them. White people call their children little monkeys and other animals often, but there is a history of White people calling Black people monkeys, and it's not a good one. Here

are some resources for further reading: https://www.nytimes.com/2018/01/08/business/hm-monkey.html. You can also read about the history of the weaponization of the term "monkey" against Black people in the United States from an educator's viewpoint here: https://www.slj.com/?detailStory=The-problem-with-picture-book-monkeys-racist-imagery-libraries.

5. Stephen Um, *1 Corinthians: The Word of the Cross* (Wheaton, IL: Crossway, 2015), 156–57.

Chapter 10: Responding Well: The Power of Words

1. The course is called Conspicuous Families and it's produced by Adoption Learning Partners. We took it in 2015, and it was dated then, but still provides some incredibly helpful information. If you'd like to check out that course and others, you can find them at: https://www.adoptionlearningpartners.org.

2. Conspicuous Families by Adoption Learning Partners, https://www.adoptionlearningpartners.org.

3. Again, this idea was something I learned from Adoption Learning Partner's Conspicuous Families course.

4. Conspicuous Families training course from: https://www.adoptionlearningpartners.org/catalog/courses/conspicuous-families.cfm.

5. Elisabeth O'Toole, *In On It: What Adoptive Parents Would Like You to Know about Adoption: A Guide for Relatives and Friends* (St. Paul, MN: Fig Press, 2011), 130.

Chapter 11: Kingdom Eyes and a Holy Imagination

1. Marlena Graves, *The Way Up Is Down: Becoming Yourself by Forgetting Yourself* (Downers Grove, IL: IVP, 2020), 146.

2. Sharon Hodde Miller, "Imagination Is Everything," *She Worships*, January 27, 2011, https://sheworships.com/imagination-is-everything/.

3. Skye Jethani, With God Daily devotional from www.SkyeJethani.com on October 29, 2020.

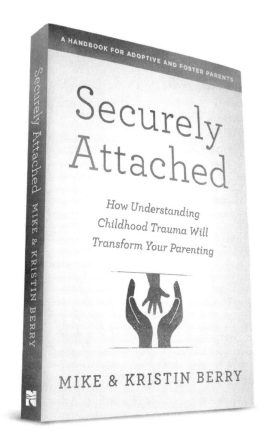